300
BUCKS
AND A
DREAM

300 BUCKS AND A DREAM

Professional and personal success on your own terms

PAT AND CRAIG RIDER

Library of Congress Control Number: 2007909343
ISBN: Hardcover   978-1-4363-0554-9
                         Softcover   978-1-4363-0553-2

This book was printed in the United States of America.

To order additional copies of this book, contact:
Xlibris Corporation
1-888-795-4274
www.Xlibris.com
Orders@Xlibris.com
44478

Contents

DEDICATION

"300 Bucks and a Dream" is dedicated to our children—John, Karen and Ashley—who bore some of the burdens and reaped the many benefits of our enterprise. Each of them contributed time and energy to the business at one time or another—answering phones, scoring assessments, assembling work books, and performing a variety of other tasks. We like to think that those experiences helped prepare them for the realities of work and life, and we're exceptionally proud of the successful adults they have become.

SPECIAL THANKS

Nancy Chifala; *NChifala@aol.com*—book cover design
Memory Lane Portraits—back cover photo
Tara Engel and Mike Jackson; Integrity Marketing—editing, advice and moral support
Dr. Dennis O'Grady, communications psychologist—advice and support

Dayton Daily News professionals including:
Dale Huffman, *dhuffman@coxohio.com*; columnist
Philip Elam, librarian
Judith Schultz, business writer
Ty Greenlee; photographer
Merideth Moss; writer

A WORD FROM
THE AUTHORS:

W e consider *300 Bucks and a Dream* to be a "hybrid book"—fitting because we have invented our own way of doing things as opposed to following an existing approach. It is an autobiography recounting the story of our business and personal lives. It is a business book revealing how we conceived, grew and nurtured our company through significant business and personal change. It's a tutorial containing advice about enjoying the successes and avoiding the pitfalls of owning a business.

Chapter One is an overview of our entire 28 years in business—with numerous personal and professional stories that have defined our career and our marriage. It is divided into several sections reflecting the stages of the development of our enterprise.

Chapters Two through Seven present the six most important lessons we have learned from our years as consultants, facilitators and business owners. These "life lessons" are relevant from both a business and personal-interest perspective. Some of the stories are humorous, some heartwarming, some inspirational. And there are a few "horror stories" we'd rather forget, but have included so others might avoid our mistakes. At the end of each of these six chapters are tips for readers as to how to strengthen their knowledge and expertise in each subject area.

Chapter Eight includes an honest assessment of our successes and shortfalls and is more in the style of a tutorial. We believe there is much to be learned from the experiences of others, so feel free to borrow our ideas.

In Chapter Nine—the final chapter—we look to the future. Although we are nearing the age when many people consider retirement, neither of us is so inclined. Our plan is to continue working at some level as long as we're having fun and others consider our work to be relevant.

Throughout the book you will find references to training terms, assessment instruments and facilitation techniques. A few of these terms may not be familiar to all readers, and are explained in the Glossary.

"300 Bucks and a Dream" is our way of sharing the joy and excitement of what we have learned—and continue to learn—from our work and from all the wonderful people who have enriched our lives. *While our stories are based on actual experiences, we do not use the names of any companies or organizations. All of the names assigned to individuals in this book are purely fictitious.*

We hope you enjoy reading about our journey as much as we have enjoyed living it. We welcome your questions and comments and encourage you to share stories about your own experiences. You can contact us at *info@ridergroup.com* and visit our website at *www.ridergroup.com*.

CHAPTER 1

Our Journey

This book is about our business—its evolution, the lessons we've learned, the groups we've worked with, and the many wonderful people we've met. It also reveals a great deal about our personal lives since the business and personal aspects of our journey are not easily separated. After all, we started our business the first year we were married and are still going strong almost thirty years later.

Our business has evolved significantly over these years as we have adapted to business realities, transitions in the marketplace, and changes in our personal needs and interests. We read many books and articles about how to start and run a business but actually did almost everything counter to what the "experts" suggested. We frequently found ourselves on the leading edge of business trends more often by following our instincts than by following someone's advice. We made our own rules as we went along yet were never rash or foolish. We could have done some things differently that might have enhanced our earnings, but nothing that would have made us richer. Most importantly, we have had the privilege of knowing thousands of incredible people who have enriched our lives, many of whom have become lifelong friends.

Things haven't always gone exactly as we might have hoped or expected, but most of the time, it has turned out better than we could have imagined. Certainly, we've had some difficult incidents and have met some unpleasant people along the way. We'll tell you about a few of those experiences. But they were insignificant in the grand scheme of things, and we chose to learn from those situations rather than to let them sap our energy or occupy our thoughts for more than a few moments. Most of our journey has been full of surprises of the very best kind.

The two of us are almost exact opposites in personality, talents, and approaches to situations, and we believe those differences make for a positive and powerful combination. At first, it took some adjusting, but it quickly became second nature for us each to anticipate how the other would react in any given situation. We have learned not to second-guess one another but to seek each other's advice. We share the same values and goals and the desire to discover and unleash the best in others. Our overriding philosophy has been to continually explore our strengths and weaknesses and to capitalize on our strengths. As Craig says, "Find out what you don't do well and *don't do it*!"

We've adjusted the focus of our work several times over the years in reaction to changes in the business world, our personal lives, and our level of excitement. But our overriding goal has remained the same—to help individuals and organizations achieve their highest potential. After much pressure from clients, friends, and even casual acquaintances, we decided to share our journey, the lessons we've learned, and some of our more interesting stories and experiences from each of our often divergent perspectives. Our hope is that you will find them interesting, enlightening and even inspirational. If *we* can live life and conduct business "on our own terms," so can you!

The Beginning

We married in the late seventies when we were both in our thirties. When we met, Craig was a single father of a four-year-old daughter. Pat was very recently divorced with a seven-year-old daughter and ten-year-old son. Craig was director of career planning and placement at a local university. Pat, who had been a stay-at-home mom for ten years, was job hunting. Our first meeting was at a "very interesting party" hosted by a mutual acquaintance.

Pat: "I was the epitome of a person living the storybook life—a husband, two kids, and a comfortable home in the suburbs, when suddenly I was "singled," and my life was turned upside down. I did what I thought was most logical. I had a teaching certificate and had been volunteering at the school my children attended, so I took the path of least resistance and signed on as a "permanent" substitute teacher. I soon found that after working with other people's children all day, I didn't have much energy left for my own. I also needed a couple of things that substitute teaching didn't provide—adult interaction and a larger, steadier income. I was desperate to find an interesting job that met those criteria, but I wasn't sure where to start since I had been out of the job market for ten years.

The party where I met Craig was an absolute disaster. I was persuaded to attend by the hostess, a casual acquaintance who was also recently divorced. I knew the moment I walked into her house that I was not vaguely interested in the wild and crazy singles scene I encountered. After less than half an hour, I was ready to go home and curl up with my cat and a good book. I made my way, literally tripping over a few drunken bodies, to the buffet table to retrieve the hors d'oeuvres I had brought. There I encountered a guy quite happily munching my crab-stuffed mushrooms.

Thinking it would be rude to pick up my tray while he was eating, I introduced myself, and we began talking. I soon realized that he was just as appalled at the surrounding chaos as I was. It was about 9:00 p.m., and after attempting to talk over the loud music, we walked outside to get away from the noise. It was a beautiful evening, and Craig was very easy to talk to. In that initial conversation I made every mistake the "single woman" books warn against, but once I started talking, I was helpless to stop. I told him all about my divorce, that I was scared, that I needed a job, that I was desperate for adult company. Most men would have run full speed in the opposite direction.

Craig was a sympathetic listener, and being a career counselor, he had wonderful advice about my job issues. He urged me to reflect about what I enjoyed and did well and then to settle on a career that fit those talents and desires. Like most people, I had never considered approaching the job hunting process from that perspective. I tucked away that information, and we moved on to other topics. He was fun and engaging, and he told great stories when I finally gave him the chance to talk. I was enthralled, and the next time I looked at my watch, it was 1:00 a.m. We reluctantly said good night, and I drove home feeling better than I had in months.

Craig had promised to call, but when I didn't hear from him the following week, I decided he was just another obnoxious male, and I pledged to stay single for the rest of my life. He finally called to make a date, and after a whirlwind romance, we married, blended a family, and started a business within the year. It was the most drastic, irresponsible, and marvelous thing I ever did in my life.

Craig: I guess meeting Pat was meant to be. I was a single father and had been living in an apartment with my daughter for nearly two years. My daughter was approaching school age, and I wanted to find a house where we could settle in. I also had the opportunity to acquire a house full of furniture from my parents who were selling their cabin in Colorado. As a college administrator, I was financially stretched, and furnishing a house would have been a challenge. My parents were going to sell the furniture if I couldn't take it quickly.

I began looking for a home near our apartment but found I couldn't afford anything close by, even in the less expensive areas of that community. Friends at work suggested I look in their neighborhood, on the other side of the city, and directed me to a house on their street that had just gone on the market. The house was a lovely Tudor—large enough to hold all the furniture I was about to acquire and priced within my budget. There was a great nursery school nearby that would be perfect for my daughter. I purchased the house and was due to move within the month.

Prior to the move, while doing some painting at the house, I met one of my neighbors. She was recently divorced and invited me to a party she was hosting. Since most of my time was spent working and caring for my four-year-old, I was not into the social scene, but I decided to attend in hopes of meeting more folks from the new neighborhood.

I quickly discovered that the party was not my style, and I spent some time observing others. Most of the guests were extremely drunk and/or on the prowl for a partner for the evening. It reminded me of a college fraternity party, and I had no interest in reviving that stage of my life. I was in the dining room sampling the various hors d'oeuvres when an attractive—and sober—woman approached the table. I happened to be eating the stuffed mushrooms that she had brought and told her how great they were. We started talking about the party and discovered we were both having a lousy time and were about ready to leave. Instead, we kept on talking.

Pat told me her story, and I gave her some input on how to conduct a successful job search. From there, we explored other topics and found we had a number of things in common—navy experience (she through her former husband), San Diego (we had both lived there at the same time), mutual friends from her college and her current neighborhood (where I'd lived before my divorce), and we were both divorced single parents.

Later in the evening, we walked down the street to look at my new house. Despite her recent bad experiences, Pat seemed to be self-assured and appeared to have her life in perspective. As we talked, all the people and the party noise faded into the background. Time just slipped away, and we discovered to our mutual surprise that it was after 1:00 a.m. I knew then I wanted to see Pat again but was caught up in packing and getting ready for the move to my new house. It was a couple weeks before our first date, but after that, we were together constantly. A few months later—much to the amazement of almost everyone—we were married and embarked on our journey to build a family and a business against incredible odds.

From the beginning, we realized that our views of the world and our operating styles were very different. Over the years, we've learned to use those differences to our clients' advantage and our own benefit. But initially, it took considerable adjustment on both our parts. The differences began to materialize a few weeks after we met.

Pat: Craig was in the process of moving, and I offered to help. We loaded up both cars, and I followed him to his new home across town—an area with which I was unfamiliar. That worked the first time, but on each consecutive trip, Craig drove a totally different route. As yet, he was unaware that I am directionally challenged and need to follow the same path several times to get my bearings. Totally frustrated after the third trip, I exited my car and asked testily, "Are you trying to make sure I won't know how to get to your house on my own?" Craig was astounded. He thought he was giving me the great gift of knowing several ways to get to his house. After a brief discussion about how differently we viewed the same scenario, we had a good laugh.

Gradually, we continued to discover the breadth and depth of those differences. Even on our honeymoon, we encountered some "interesting challenges."

Craig: I was an avid sailor and had been in the boating business when I lived on the East Coast, so I suggested that a week-long honeymoon cruise would be a great adventure. Pat's only experience on a sailboat was a brief one-hour sail many years before, but she thought that it sounded like a wonderful romantic adventure. Visions of Bing Crosby and Grace Kelly in True Love *came to her mind. We waited several months after our wedding as we wanted to get our children settled before we left them for any length of time.*

We rented a twenty-eight-foot sailboat—quite adequate for the two of us—and sailed out of Greenport, Long Island. The first morning started out just fine. We had a pretty good wind, and it was a beautiful sunny day. We were heading for Block Island, which was visible in the distance. Pat thought the fact that she could see our destination meant that it was going to be a short sail. Unfortunately, the wind died, and the trip took almost nine hours. While I was perfectly fine "enjoying the journey," I soon discovered that Pat was much more interested in "reaching the destination." We made many more interesting discoveries during that week about the different ways we respond to the same situations. Those discoveries provided ample opportunity for discussion at the time and great stories for future enjoyment.

The Dream

While SLOWLY sailing the ocean blue, we had lots of time to talk about the future. Both of our fathers had owned their own businesses, and we began exploring that possibility for ourselves. Craig's work as director of career planning and placement at the university limited him to counseling students or alumni, but he had been getting phone calls from people outside the university who had heard about his approach to job hunting and were seeking his advice. Pat's new job as administrative manager for a small engineering company was providing a modest but steady second income. Craig had just taught an evening course at the university earning $300 for his efforts, which seemed like a lot of "extra cash" to us at the time. Armed with those resources and lots of ideas, we began dreaming about starting a business of our own, helping others with their career issues.

We made two promises to ourselves while on that sailboat and have kept those promises to this day. We pledged never to put any more of our own money into our business beyond that initial $300 and never to borrow any money for business purposes. With those promises in mind, Career Resources was born; and over the next few months, we made some progress toward our dream. We located a secretarial service near our home to answer our phone line, collect our mail, and do some typing as needed for a grand total of $6 a month. We ordered letterhead and business cards and began telling a few people about our new venture although at this point, it was more of an *adventure*.

Craig: I began taking appointments in the evenings with people who needed career counseling and job hunting skills but didn't qualify for the university program. There was a lot of interest surfacing for this new approach to determining a career path that fits a person's skills and interests versus settling for whatever job that happens to be available. When I had a client appointment, Pat would retreat upstairs with the three kids and try to keep them quiet—not an easy task since they didn't necessarily want to be together at all, let alone in close quarters. It's safe to say that our family situation at that time bore little resemblance to **The Brady Bunch.**

In addition to those evening appointments, we soon developed a seminar for teachers who were interested in changing careers. It was a time when there was a wealth of teachers looking for jobs and few teaching positions available. We advertised our seminar in the newspaper on the same page as the employment ads and received many responses. The Saturday seminars were held in a downtown hotel and covered such topics as skill identification, alternative careers, resume writing, and job hunting skills. It also featured a panel of former teachers who had made the transition to new careers. We offered all of that information, plus materials, lunch, and free parking for the low, low price of $50. We packed people in week after week, and our tiny business bank account began to grow.

Word of Craig's career counseling expertise started to spread, and several local organizations contacted him to present job hunting seminars for folks that were being downsized. Downsizing was a new term in the late '70s for an anomaly that soon turned into an all-too-frequent reality for many employees of the large companies and manufacturing operations in our area of the country. Craig was also contacted to participate in facilitating a program in Detroit for a major utility company that was cutting its workforce significantly. He took vacation time to work with that project, adding to his expertise and reputation in this new field. In the meantime, Pat found herself unemployed when the company she worked for lost some major government contracts and went out of business.

It was the perfect time for us to become serious about implementing our dream. We found a nice single office in a downtown bank building as the headquarters for Career Resources. It had an adjoining junk room that had no access to the hallway and was in sore need of a coat of paint and a major cleanup. Craig negotiated with the building manager to rent that second room for storage, knowing that the square footage cost for storage was a fraction of the cost of regular office space. The building manager agreed to rent the second room for a few dollars per square foot. After we signed the lease, he asked Craig what we would be storing in that room. Craig answered, "A conference table, some chairs, and a credenza." The building manager just smiled. His office was next to ours, and he seemed to enjoy our enthusiasm as well as the fact that we painted and spruced up the place. None of us could foresee that within a couple of years we would be leasing almost an entire floor of the building for our thriving outplacement business.

Pat: Craig and I both have the knack and desire to acquire high quality objects for bargain basement prices. I shopped the office furniture stores and found a beautiful conference table that had been specially ordered but never purchased. I was able to negotiate a great deal for the table and then bargained for a set of leather chairs to complete the set. With a desk and a few other pieces from home, we furnished a very comfortable and professional-looking office. Craig found a clever way to purchase gently used office equipment from the university as items went up for bids each year-end. We added typewriters and a copy machine from that source.

While Pat worked to establish the business, Craig took appointments whenever he could—most of the time during evenings or vacation days. We were still struggling to clearly define the focus of our business. Craig had ample skills and experience in the career planning arena—a relatively new concept that was being embraced mainly by universities. A few corporations were offering career planning internally to develop career paths for key employees, but that trend was in its infancy and wasn't popular enough to sustain a business.

Craig did a lot of testing and assessment work at the university to help students determine their skills and career interests. A national testing service took notice and contacted us to do occupational assessments for individuals being considered for hiring or promotion. Those paper and pencil assessments predicted a person's likelihood of success in certain types of jobs. We started conducting occupational testing and counseling for that organization on a regular basis as part of Career Resources' offerings.

We also rented some of our office space to two individuals who conducted assessments and did counseling on a part-time basis. They worked with injured workers contracted through the state workers compensation bureau. The results of those assessments determined what jobs would be appropriate for individuals who, due to injury, could no longer perform their current work. Their expertise in the realm of assessment, added to our own, led us to consider establishing an assessment center as the key focus of our business.

We had already proven we were adept at running workshops, and that was yet another alternative for our business focus. Pat attended a training session and became credentialed to teach time management and stress management workshops. We incorporated some of that information into our career planning workshop agendas, which we marketed to area businesses.

A Golden Opportunity

While we were deciding which of these varied services to incorporate into our fledgling business, a major transformation was taking place in the business world. The era of downsizing was sweeping through the country with a vengeance. Wave after wave of loyal employees—many in their fifties who had worked with one company their entire lives—were marched into human resources offices and handed their walking papers. Few companies were offering any job-finding assistance to the employees they dismissed.

We began hearing one horror story after another from folks who had lost their jobs. One company lined up all their employees outside the human resources department and called them in one by one. Upon entering the office, each person was given a sheet of colored paper with directions as to what their fate would be. As they left the office, they were holding either a blue sheet, which meant they had retained their job with a reduction in pay, or a pink sheet, which outlined their severance benefits. Of course the folks standing in line awaiting their own fate soon learned the significance of the two colors. Such inhumane practices stunned loyal employees, most of whom had invested years of their lives at a single organization.

Pat: The downsizing mania presented the focus and an incredible opportunity for us and our new venture. Craig had the perfect skills and credentials. He was well known in the community for his work in counseling and placing students in appropriate careers and for the job hunting workshops he had developed and presented at the university and to the general public. And we both had the ability, temperament, and desire to provide a caring, structured environment in which people could deal with such a life-changing event.

Craig began receiving calls from company human resource directors, asking him to conduct job hunting workshops for professional and hourly workers who were facing unemployment. After months of uncertainty and indecision as to what services Career Resources might offer, it became obvious that we would soon be immersed in the downsizing decade of the '80s. The big question was whether Craig should take the risk of leaving his job at the university with no other steady means of income. At that point, we had no way of knowing how extensive the downsizing trend would become.

Pat: Once again, an opportunity presented itself. I was approached to become the administrative and financial manager for the local office of an international accounting firm. It was a challenging and exciting prospect with lots of professional development opportunities, and the compensation was beyond my expectations. That job offer made it possible for Craig to leave his university position and establish Career Resources as one of the first outplacement companies in the Dayton area. My salary supported the family adequately, and we saved every penny that came into the business for the next three years.

Throughout the early '80s, Career Resources was one of very few organizations in the community offering the full range of outplacement services that were so much in demand. As the work kept pouring in, we continued acquiring additional office space adjacent to our original location until we occupied most of the twelfth floor of the building. After three years of steady business expansion—with no end in sight—Pat left the accounting firm and came to Career Resources full-time. That made it possible for us to open a satellite office in the nearby town of Troy as well as an on-site office at a large manufacturing organization that was substantially cutting its workforce over a period of several years.

For the executives and managers of companies that were downsizing, the new vocabulary term was "outplacement"—a more refined term for losing one's job. While the phenomenon started mainly in the manufacturing sector, it came to encompass every industry throughout the decade of the '80s. Executive outplacement packages, offered to the highest level of employees, often included extensive services such as individual counseling, office space, secretarial support, and job hunting guidance for extended periods of time—usually until the person located new employment.

The good news was that since downsizing was a new phenomenon, many companies felt guilty and offered their terminated employees generous severance packages. Typically, managers and executives received some level of outplacement counseling, and many of them received full services. Our executive package included individual office space within our complex where individuals conducted their job search and received personal attention. We provided telephones, full secretarial support, and all the amenities they had become accustomed to at their previous employment. Our technical assistance included career assessment, resume writing, cover letter development, interview training, database searches, networking leads, and endless advice and attention.

Craig: We naturally became close friends and confidants of the individuals who came "to work" at our offices each day. Many had been employed with their companies for decades and felt betrayed and discarded. Our job was to help them close that chapter of their lives and focus on the future as quickly and effectively as possible, and in some cases, that was a daunting task. One weekend Pat spent several hours on the phone with a client who was considering suicide. We got professional help for her, and fortunately, she was able to regain her equilibrium.

We also maintained very close relationships with our client companies. Especially at the beginning of the outplacement onslaught, many organizations agonized over the decisions they had to make in reaction to business realities. We worked closely with management to make sure the process was carried out as humanely as possible and in a manner that assured that the company would not be in legal jeopardy. But after a few years, downsizing became commonplace, and those attitudes began to change. Many organizations replaced their experienced executive teams with people whose focus was primarily on bottom-line issues. These new folks didn't have the close ties with existing employees and were less inclined to spend money on outplacement packages.

Whatever the company's attitude, we walked a tightrope between loyalty to the company that hired us and loyalty to the individuals we were assisting. We were able to do that by maintaining the strictest confidentiality in regard to the company and genuine concern for each individual we assisted. Throughout our many years in the business, not one of our outplacement clients filed a lawsuit against a former employer despite a strong nationwide trend in that direction.

During this time, we came to recognize an interesting pattern that almost certainly signaled an impending reorganization. The company would hire a new vice president or director of human resources from another area of the country. The new executive was advised to reside in a community somewhat removed from the location of company headquarters. That strategy made it less likely that the HR person would run into disgruntled former employees at the local grocery store or shopping center. When a client company informed us that a new HR person was coming on board, we knew to begin gearing up for the inevitable.

In some special circumstances, we tried our hardest to persuade companies to exempt certain individuals—even if temporarily—from the groups that were targeted for layoffs. If an employee or someone in the immediate family was seriously ill, we urged the company to spare their job, at least for the time being. That advice was often ignored by people in the personnel office who tended to be list oriented. So we occasionally dealt with heart-wrenching stories such as a man who was dismissed soon after his mother died and just after finding out his wife was critically ill, and a person who was contacted during his family vacation in Disneyland and informed by phone that his job was being eliminated. One of our clients was even terminated via a message on his voice mail.

Pat: Craig has a natural ability to connect with people and make them feel good about themselves regardless of the circumstances. So meeting new clients who had just been informed of their dismissal was one of his key responsibilities, and his approach was artful. Within an hour, he could usually convince a new client that this was an opportunity to discover exactly what he or she loved doing and the perfect time to find a job that would be much more satisfying than the one they had been forced to leave. He helped clients determine the best way to break the news to their families and made sure they knew we would provide every resource needed to conduct an effective job search and find a new position quickly. We even offered to meet with spouses and other family members to allay their fears and help them understand how to be most helpful during the job search process.

Every person who came to one of our offices to conduct a job hunt was welcomed as part of our "family." We're proud to say that, with the exception of one person who had a problem with alcoholism, every one of the "outplaced" individuals we worked with found appropriate new employment. Most of them found positions that were much more satisfying and compatible with their talents and desires than the positions they were forced to leave. We've kept in touch with many former clients, and years later, these individuals consider their outplacement experience one of the most positive events of their lives.

Pat: We soon learned that one of the most valuable assets we could offer our clients was access to the very different skill sets and styles of communicating that Craig and I had to offer. If the client needed to look for possibilities, expand their thinking as to their next career move, or generate new networking opportunities, they would consult with Craig. His ideas and enthusiasm were limitless. If they needed to focus, organize, or develop resumes and cover letters, they came to me.

Using a wide variety of assessment tools, we determined what vocations, jobs, and even what companies would be the best fit for each of our outplacement clients. Most of them had fallen into jobs without taking time to discover what they really did well and enjoyed doing. Many had been promoted from jobs that suited them well to ones that didn't match their talents. As Craig noted, these folks had opted for "taking the path of least resistance versus the one of greatest opportunity." It was a real ego boost for them to be able to explore, determine, and verbalize the areas in which they excelled. They were excited and energized to think that they could actually find new employment doing something they loved to do.

We used those same assessment tools ourselves to determine our roles within the company and even within the community. We soon found that our differences gave us a huge advantage in making contacts and developing business opportunities. Our encounter with the human resources director for a large banking institution was a perfect example. For months, we had tried unsuccessfully to arrange a meeting with him to explain our services. Craig, being the persistent one, finally got him to agree to spend fifteen minutes with us. Fred set the meeting time for 11:45 a.m. at his office—a not so subtle indication that he intended to terminate the conversation by claiming he had a luncheon appointment.

Pat: When we entered Fred's office, he seated us in guest chairs near the door and retreated behind his desk, which was a good twelve feet away. We practically had to shout to interact. As we began to describe our business and our philosophy of working with clients, it was obvious that he related more to me. My style is to get straight to the point and say what needs to be said with few extraneous remarks. Craig, who loves to tell stories and engage on a more personal level, saw what was happening from the very beginning. He let my interaction with Fred proceed with few interjections or additional comments. Within a few minutes, Fred scooted his chair from behind his desk and came closer to us. He continued to move his chair closer as the conversation proceeded, finally joining us in a cozy circle.

Seeing that our fifteen minutes had elapsed, we started to wrap up our comments and prepare to leave. Surprisingly, Fred invited us to join him for lunch. His interest continued to grow, and after a lengthy lunch, he asked to come see our offices. When he finally left at 2:30 p.m., we had established a very pleasant relationship.

The more we interacted with our outplacement clients, the more we came to understand how inappropriately some companies treated their managers— even to the degree of pitting them against each other. Joe and George were outplaced from a large health care organization. Joe had been at our offices for a couple of weeks when he heard that George had been downsized and would be working with us as well. Joe indicated that the two of them did not get along at all, and he didn't want to have any contact with George. We were able to accommodate by assigning them to offices in different areas of our complex.

At first, they avoided each other completely, spending most of their time in their respective offices behind closed doors. Then we noticed they would occasionally stop to converse if they met in the hallway. A couple of weeks later, they arranged to have lunch together, and soon they were spending a lot of time encouraging each other and even sharing job leads. Eventually, much to our amazement, they announced that they were going into business together.

While helping Joe and George write their business plan and establish their new enterprise, we asked them what had prompted the transformation from one of open hostility to a warm and enthusiastic partnership. They explained that the environment at their former place of work had encouraged mistrust between departments. There was competition for what was perceived as limited resources and rewards. And there was little sharing of information with the rest of the executive team by either the CEO or CFO.

In addition to a divisive work situation, Joe and George had very different operating styles. Rather than viewing individual differences as positive and building a team that thrived on diverse styles, their leader tried to force the entire management group into the same mold. Later, when the decision was made to downsize, Joe and George were the first to go since the leader's perception was that they "didn't play by the rules."

We helped Joe and George understand that their differences were a plus in a working relationship. While Joe loved to manage the details, George had the long-range vision and enjoyed the sales process. As they planned their new business they realized that each could utilize his natural strengths. It was heartening to watch their confidence and enthusiasm grow as they developed their business plan and launched what ultimately became a very successful enterprise. We couldn't help but think that their former employer had missed a great opportunity to combine their differences into a powerful working relationship.

Pat: We have dozens of stories about how empowering it is for individuals to discover what they do well and love doing. Perspectives about work totally change, and energy and spirits soar. It was inspirational for Craig and me to observe the great things people accomplished when they grasped that knowledge about themselves and were released from the negative politics of their former work environment.

The career development piece of our business also became important for organizations that wanted to retain and develop employees and make the most of their talents. One very forward-looking company asked us to design a career development program for their entire organization. This pet food manufacturer was in its infancy but was growing at a steady rate. Once we experienced the corporate culture firsthand, it was easy to understand why. At the time we began working with them they had fewer than two hundred employees at their corporate headquarters and a couple of small manufacturing plants in rural areas around the country. Every employee was treated as an important member of the team, whether he or she was an executive or a line worker. The CEO visited every location each quarter and spoke directly to all employees. He made a point of knowing each person by name.

Pat: The career development program we designed for this company included several career and personality assessments, a group workshop, and a one-on-one follow-up meeting with each participant. To this day, we consider it to be one of the most satisfying projects we ever designed and implemented. When we were developing the workshop with the human resources vice president, we asked if he was concerned that some folks might utilize the information they received to seek a position elsewhere. He said that the company truly wanted each employee to be happy in their position. If the ideal job wasn't available internally, the company would prefer the person leave with positive feelings rather than stay in a job that wasn't satisfying. That attitude was—and still is—rare, but it served the company well. A survey conducted five years after the inception of the career development program showed that almost 80 percent of the individuals who completed the program were able to contribute at a higher level (defined as either accepting a promotion or taking on additional responsibilities within the company) versus only 30 percent of employees who had not participated in the program.

Almost without exception, every employee in that organization loved working there and revered the president. The positive regard permeated corporate headquarters, every department, and every plant no matter how remote. While conducting one of our seminars during the third shift, a production worker was injured on the line. The plant manager was on-site within minutes and rode with the employee when the ambulance took him to the hospital. He also called the family to make sure they had someone to stay with the children so the wife could get to the hospital. Fortunately, the injury was not serious. That incident epitomized the respect and concern that management felt for every employee throughout the organization, and that feeling was reciprocated. It was our great privilege to work with that company and watch it grow and prosper.

We especially enjoyed our trips to the remote manufacturing plants because the people were so enthusiastic and anxious to learn. Many individuals who worked in the Nebraska plant also owned farms. They farmed during the day and worked second shift. The fact that the company had located there made it possible for these workers to keep their farms while earning a good living. Everyone there had wonderful small town values and an incredible work ethic. They considered us the "consultants from the big city" since the population of their town was only a few thousand.

Craig: I'm sure they considered me even more of a city slicker during one of the training programs we conducted. I was using an overhead projector and was accustomed to training rooms where the image was projected onto a dry-erase board. At one point early in the program, I was using a colored marker to underline a particular item I wanted to emphasize. There was an audible gasp from the group. I turned to look at the board and realized that I was writing on the nicely painted white wall of the conference room rather than on a dry-erase board. Much to my relief, the marker was not the permanent type, and I was able to wash the wall clean.

By this point Career Resources had three offices, and we were frequently on the road conducting programs like the one just described. It became evident that we were in dire needed of additional professional employees. Craig was running the downtown office, which was filled to capacity with twelve to fifteen executive outplacement clients in residence. He also conducted group programs and many outplacement workshops. Pat was dividing her time between the satellite office and an on-site job center for a large client. Our administrative people were very capable, but we were in need of folks who could work with the clients on their job search efforts, especially when we were out of town.

As adept as we were at helping others make career choices and transitions, we were not very skilled at hiring our own professional staff. It was difficult to find employees that had the skills and knowledge to do the job the way we wanted it done, especially since outplacement was a relatively new field. Also, we tended to see the potential in candidates rather than the probability of them living up to that potential. To add to that problem, our existing corporate clients were used to dealing directly with us, and they didn't want that to change. Due to our own operating styles, it was easier for us to see the potential in people than it was for us to discern their possible shortcomings. That caused us to make a number of poor hiring decisions. And none of the professionals we hired over the years were successful at developing new business.

As much as we needed additional staff, there was also reluctance on our part to shoulder a large payroll. We remembered our promise to never borrow money, and a significant expansion of staff would have necessitated a loan. Because of those considerations, we often hired people on a consulting basis— an approach that was less than ideal. In one situation, we learned that our consultant had actually approached a major client in an attempt to *underbid us* and steal the business. Obviously, that breach of confidence required immediate termination of our consulting relationship with the person.

Pat: Neither of us liked handling those situations the few times we had to dismiss someone. Because of all our outplacement work, we were keenly aware of the negative effects of losing a job. Fortunately, we seldom needed to terminate an employee, but when it was necessary, that duty usually fell to me since I tend to be more direct in my approach. However, in one such case, Craig decided that it was only fair that he shoulder the responsibility for once. So he asked Lou to join us in the conference room and started the conversation. Since he has such a difficult time delivering bad news, Craig began the conversation by reviewing all the positive things Lou had accomplished. It was obvious to me that, given all the praise, Lou was starting to think he was getting a raise. I finally interrupted and informed him that we wouldn't have need of his services any longer. From that time forward, employee dismissal was part of my permanent job description.

Despite our large work load and our occasional problems with staffing, we were determined to maintain some semblance of a balanced life. A third promise we made to ourselves on our honeymoon cruise was to never become totally consumed with the business to the detriment of our personal lives. We had a blended family of three children who didn't particularly want to be living together, and that issue required a lot of our emotional energy. It was challenging to leave the office after a day of helping clients who were going through emotional adjustments and return home to children who were doing the same. Our solution was to insist on some "decompression time" each day when we returned home.

One of the greatest gifts we ever gave each other was the purchase of a Jacuzzi spa, which was installed outside on our deck. It was a firm rule that, after we got home and greeted the kids, we had twenty to thirty minutes alone in the Jacuzzi to talk over the day and relax. After that, our attention belonged to the kids and to each other. We tried never to address our business issues the rest of the evening, and with few exceptions, we were able to follow that rule. The division of labor at home was as equal as it was at work. Both of us cooked, cleaned, and parented—and held on to our sanity most of the time!

New Possibilities

In the late '80s, several things happened that gradually shifted the focus of our business. First of all, Craig accepted a key role in redeveloping our city's community leadership program. The chamber of commerce sponsored an annual ten-month program for current and emerging leaders from corporate, government, and not-for-profit organizations. The goal of Leadership Dayton was to familiarize participants with the systems that made the community function and to encourage these leaders to work toward enhancing these systems as well as to get involved on nonprofit community boards. Once a month, the thirty-five to forty participants spent an entire day studying a particular topic, such as local government, education, or human services. They also made on-site visits to some of the organizations that impacted the topic area and interacted with experts in the field.

The program—one of the first leadership programs in the country—had been in existence for about twelve years. While very effective it also was in need of a bit of a facelift. Craig, the program director, and a few of the program alumni were members of a task force that developed recommendations for changes and enhancements. One of the most exciting changes for Craig was the addition of an opening retreat.

Craig: When I had participated in the leadership program, the retreat came in the middle of the ten-month period, and it turned out to be more of an academic lecture series than a chance for the participants to discuss and assess community issues among ourselves. At our retreat, I realized that most of the class members still didn't know each other's names. We had each introduced ourselves at the beginning of the program, but there had never been the opportunity to spend time really getting to know each other. The day-long programs were totally consumed listening to speakers and visiting sites relevant to the month's topic.

As a result of participating in the program, it was expected that participants would get excited about how they might affect the issues important to the community. That was happening to a certain extent, but the chamber and alumni board wanted to enhance the program's benefit to the community. The committee determined such an outcome would be much more likely if participants really got to know each other at the beginning of the program and learned to work together as a cohesive team. I had heard about an outdoor adventure program in the area and arranged for a group of alumni to spend a day sampling that program to see if it might work as an opening retreat for the next group of leadership program participants.

There were many aspects of that adventure program that appealed to the committee and especially to Craig from a team building perspective. As a result, a two-day retreat was added to the leadership program curriculum as the opening event. Craig was asked to cofacilitate that experience along with members of the staff of the adventure facility.

Pat: I was also involved in this new adventure although it was not in my realm of experience and seemed a bit too free flowing for my nature. Experiential programming includes activities that require both physical and mental problem solving. Even though an activity may be contrived, people react much the same under these circumstances as they do when pressured to complete a task in a real-life situation. Issues arise that need to be facilitated on the spot, and valuable conversations take place among the participants. The lessons learned are easily transferable to real-world interactions in all types of situations.

I much prefer a more traditional, planned program so I can be prepared well ahead of time. Planning is one of my strengths and has always been one of my key responsibilities in the company. I am very good at developing outlines, agendas, materials, and handouts to enhance the learning experience. But since we had never facilitated a program like this one, I had nothing to refer to in preparation for that first experiential retreat.

Craig: Pat began asking me several months before that first leadership program to give her some idea of the kinds of handouts and materials we would need so she could start preparing. Quite frankly, I didn't have a clue, but I didn't share that with Pat. I knew in general what activities and discussions would be included, but I hadn't yet gotten my "inspiration" that would tie all the components together. I am truly most effective under pressure and motivated to do my best at the last moment. I knew about Pat's need for up-front planning and tried to accommodate, but I was still waiting for my moment of inspiration.

Pat: This went on for several months. Before we knew it, it was the final week before the retreat, and we still had no agenda, no materials, and I had no idea how this very important program with forty community leaders was going to proceed. Craig and I were having lunch with a client across the street from our offices when I became aware of my heart pounding and I started to feel faint. I apologized to the client and told Craig I needed to get back to the office because I wasn't feeling well. He said he would be along soon. I said, "You don't understand. I need to go immediately and YOU need to come with me!"

I'm not sure how we made it across the street to our building. By the time we got into the elevator, I was hyperventilating and could barely stand up. We asked the elevator attendant, whom we knew well from our many years in the building, to please get us to our floor quickly without making any stops on the way. When we reached our offices, I lay down on the couch and tried to relax. I don't much like anyone to fuss over me, but I finally admitted that I needed help, and Craig called the emergency squad. When they arrived, my heart rate was 220 and irregular, and I ended up in the hospital. The diagnosis was tachycardia and arrhythmia—brought on by stress or, as Craig likes to say, "brought on by the lack of a plan!"

Craig: Fortunately Pat was fine after some medication and a bit of rest. Believe me, that evening I developed a plan for the program, which by then was only three days away! Ever since that incident, I am sure to have a written plan for every program, especially for the ones Pat and I facilitate together. I claim that if I should keel over in the middle of a program, Pat can just drag me over to a corner and continue with the agenda.

The leadership retreat was a huge success. We utilized some assessment tools including the Myers-Briggs Type Indicator (MBTI) and a leadership style assessment to help participants determine how they could be most effective both in their work lives and volunteer positions. We blended those tools with plenty of large and small group discussions and some components of the outdoor adventure experience. By the end of the two-day retreat, all forty participants knew each other's names and had begun to work together as a team to solve problems. That transformed the remainder of the ten-month leadership program as the class members studied about and tackled issues within the community. It also maintained their effectiveness and closeness after their program year concluded. Twenty years later, Craig is still facilitating the opening leadership retreats.

After initiating many community leadership retreats, we began getting requests from participants wanting similar experiences for their own corporate teams. That eventually led us into a whole new phase of our business and the opportunity to work with all types and sizes of organizations and corporate groups.

During that time, one of our client companies approached us about developing a program for employees who had kept their jobs during the period of severe downsizing. Those employees not only were shell-shocked by what had happened to their coworkers, but they now had to perform essentially the same workload with half the number of workers. In many organizations, morale and trust were at an all time low.

Craig: I determined the most important approach was to help the remaining employees work together more effectively and understand and support each other. This was the beginning of our extensive work with corporate teams which continues today. Some of the assessment instruments we used for years with our outplacement clients worked equally as well with the team building and leadership development programs. The MBTI helped our outplacement clients determine their strengths and ways to apply them. When used with groups, it is invaluable in demonstrating the strengths of each individual team member as well as highlighting ways the group can capitalize on those strengths. By combining the Myers-Briggs Type Indicator (MBTI), Leadership Practices Inventory (LPI), and a variety of problem solving activities, we created one-, two-, and three-day programs for corporations. The development and success of team building programs started us down a path that would soon transform our company.

For the next few years, we maintained three office sites, six full-time employees, various consultants on retainer, and a couple of our kids—now teenagers—who helped score assessments for our outplacement clients, career development programs, and team program participants. We were stretched pretty thin but were truly enjoying the work.

While Craig had facilitated the opening retreats for Leadership Dayton since 1987, six years later, the chamber of commerce asked us to develop and facilitate the entire ten-month program in addition to the opening and closing retreats. This was a perfect match for Pat's skills. She loves to design and lead structured programs, creating a welcoming atmosphere for both the presenters and the program participants. Soon afterward, we took on two other regional leadership programs; and in 2000, we added the statewide leadership program to the list. Over the years, we received recognition for our efforts winning both Ohio and international awards for programming excellence.

Pat: In the early '90s, I also worked with a large corporation with worldwide locations to design and provide counseling and job hunting services for trailing spouses. In competing for the most talented employees, this organization realized that many of the young managers they wished to attract from other companies, or relocate within their own ranks, had working spouses. The trailing spouse program was an added benefit that sometimes tipped the scale in getting employees to transfer or to join their company. It was a natural extension of the outplacement work we did— using the same instruments to discover strengths and styles, developing resumes, and using our extensive network for referrals.

At that time, a venture capital firm contacted us about heading up an umbrella company that would include outplacement, personnel, job placement, and testing services. While it was an appealing offer that encompassed many of our areas of expertise, there were several things that held us back. First of all, we were concerned about the possibility of at least the appearance of a conflict of interest by getting paid for both outplacement and for placing individuals in new jobs. Secondly, we both loved the interaction with our clients. Under the proposed configuration, we would be managing a large organization rather than actually spending one-on-one time with our clients. Even more of a concern was the fact that we would be managing a large staff of employees. We had proven to ourselves (and probably to a few former employees) that hiring and managing people was not our forte at this time in our lives even though we had both been successful at it in former jobs. For those and other reasons, we decided to discontinue those discussions.

Companies were still purging throughout the early '90s although their feelings of guilt had diminished significantly. Downsizing was no longer an anomaly but an expectation, and companies offered fewer and fewer services to all but the very top echelon of employees. In our area, a couple of regional outplacement firms had entered the picture. Competition was increasing as fees and levels of service decreased, but we had been able to hold our own since we were well known in the community and had a reputation for providing very personalized service.

Then the inevitable happened. A national outplacement firm moved into town. Their strategy was to underbid the local firms—in many cases by half—in order to drive out the competition. After losing out to them on several large outplacement projects, we had some tough decisions to make. As a small company that refused to downgrade services in order to win jobs, the choice was actually a fairly easy one.

Our team, leadership, and career development programs were continuing to grow. And, after a dozen years of helping folks who were in the throes of dealing with job loss and sharing the pain that goes with it, we were ready for a change. We were also anxious to simplify our lives by divesting ourselves of multiple offices and numerous employees and consultants.

Craig: We had been talking with a regional outplacement firm for several months about the possibility of a merger but decided to change gears and see if they were interested in purchasing the outplacement piece of our business. After several meetings, an agreement was reached. The purchasing company would pay us a percentage of the income they received from our former corporate clients for a period of three years. The purchasing firm took over the lease of our satellite office and even hired some of our administrative staff. They also purchased most of our furniture and fixtures at both the remote site and our expanded downtown site.

We transferred the outplaced individuals from our offices to the offices of the purchasing firm. We introduced the organizations that utilized our outplacement services to the purchasing firm's management staff. In hindsight, we would have structured that deal differently. Our agreement brought us very little cash in lieu of receiving a percentage of the fees the purchasing company brought in from our former clients. It was soon evident that in the absence of the strong relationships we had established with our client companies and the lack of personalized attention given to the outplaced individuals, our former clients decided to shop around for the lowest prices. By the end of the first year, the purchasing company had lost most of our former clients, and our revenue from that source was minimal.

Taking the Plunge

Even though outplacement services had been providing about 70 percent of our revenue, we were confident we could make up the difference pretty quickly. We decided to change the company name since the name Career Resources no longer accurately reflected our business focus. Many people were familiar with the Rider name, so we decided to keep it simple and christened our corporation The Rider Group. With a new name, a smaller office suite and only two employees, we embarked on a new phase of our business and our personal lives.

The corporate team building business was really catching on, and we were one of very few companies in our area that offered customized team building programs—with or without the adventure component. Also, we were unique in the fact that we could incorporate one or more of a number of assessment instruments in the design of a program. The assessment piece meant that teams came away with a deeper understanding of the unique strengths of each member of their team as well as practical ways to integrate those strengths into the team design.

We also found ourselves in a new place personally. Our three children were on their own, and we had total freedom for the first time in our marriage. Our team and career development programs took us all over the continent, and our experiences were both enjoyable and enlightening. Our accommodations varied from the luxury of the Hotel Del Coronado to the down-home atmosphere of Chet & Emils—a combination motel, bar, restaurant and bowling alley that doubled as a venue for wedding receptions when they placed floorboards over the bowling lanes.

One engagement took us to Canada where we did a half-day program for an association of construction companies. The organization was in transition and was changing to a new focus and structure. We designed a special activity for them, which included breaking the group into teams to build bridges out of materials such as paper plates, Styrofoam cups, paper clips, rubber bands, etc. This building activity signified the energy and resourcefulness it would take to successfully complete the transition and stay energized until the next meeting. We had all of these building materials in a trunk, which was duly inspected at the US/Canadian border.

Pat: The border guard was quite interested in the contents of our trunk and began asking questions about the purpose of bringing those items with us. Craig, always anxious to interact and share information, attempted to explain in detail what we were going to do with our trunk full of goodies. I was trying to get his attention to warn him to stop talking. I had heard that the Canadians were not particularly fond of consultants from the United States doing work in their country, and I feared we might be hassled or detained if they realized we were on a consulting gig. The guard, who was obviously not familiar with the concept of team building and was confused by Craig's lengthy explanation, finally said, "It looks like you're planning a giant picnic!" I quickly answered, "Yes, that's exactly what we're doing" and nudged Craig so that he would end his potentially trouble-causing explanation.

That program was fun for everyone and provided terrific benefits for the association. In addition to leading several outdoor activities, we designed an event where the participants built incredibly elaborate bridges with those "picnic supplies"! One group constructed a working drawbridge complete with a drawbridge operator built to scale. A participant shared that he had been attending the conferences for years and had met more people, made more contacts, and gotten to know people better in three hours than in all the past years of attendance.

The venue was beautiful too—a lovely lodge and conference center a couple hours north of Toronto. The only drawback was that the lodge had quite an infestation of mice. At night, when all was quiet, you could hear them scurrying up and down inside the walls. Neither of us got much sleep that night.

We traveled to a number of interesting and scenic places, leading programs for a large manufacturer of sporting goods equipment with multiple divisions. Most of their employees were young, enthusiastic, and energetic and preferred high adventure programs with lots of physical activity. For one of their divisions, we booked a camp-and-ropes course in a remote and mountainous part of Colorado. Fortunately, we decided to rent a four-wheel drive vehicle despite the fact that it was May. The camp was located well up a mountainside, and about a mile from our destination, we encountered a frozen stream. Our car got us through the ice without a hitch, but most of the program participants were not so fortunate. Many had to traverse the last mile on foot, carrying their luggage and supplies. They took it in stride, considering the trek as just another part of the adventure.

The four-day agenda included both indoor and outdoor programming. It was a very engaged and enthusiastic group, and they enjoyed and learned from every experience. One of the most humorous events occurred as team members tried to scale a ten-foot wooden wall with a goal of getting everyone safely to the other side. They weren't having much luck when a participant boldly suggested that someone should donate a pair of jeans to the cause so the team could use them as a climbing rope. Much to everyone's surprise, one young woman readily accepted the challenge and began removing her jeans to donate to the cause. She had on a very attractive pair of flowered thermal long johns, but her gesture still prompted lots of cheering and a good bit of interest from the guys. The group managed to scale the wall without using the jeans except perhaps as an incentive.

Pat: There was no plumbing at this camp. All the hot water was supplied by a solar heating tank, and each evening we lined up for our showers (two minutes per person, and everyone was counting) in the outdoor shower stalls. The only bathroom facilities were outhouses, and in the middle of the night, I needed to use those facilities. I tried in vain to get Craig to accompany me on the quarter-mile trek, so I bundled up, grabbed a flashlight, and walked alone. On my way back, I heard an animal come crashing through the woods and saw a large dark figure headed right for me. In that moment of sheer terror, I recalled reading an article about a bear attack. The person survived, but her most vivid memory was of how horrible the bear smelled. Being a bit of a neat freak, my first thoughts were focused more on the fear of the unpleasant odor than on the impending attack. You can imagine how relieved I was when I recognized the camp owner's black Labrador retriever. He was very happy to see someone up and around at 2:00 a.m., and I was incredibly happy to see him! He accompanied me back to the cabin.

Craig: This four-day program was one of our all-time favorites. The entire team was wonderful—engaged and enthusiastic no matter what (even when carrying their luggage up a steep ice-covered hill). The president was a delightful person, completely unassuming. He considered himself a part of the gang. When it was time for cleanup after meals, he was the first one at the outdoor sink, scraping plates and washing dishes. He waited in line for his shower just like everyone else. His positive attitude permeated the entire management team, and they made great strides in enhancing their ability to work together while having a great time.

As our team building work continued to grow, the focus began to change. While the outdoor and adventure components of team building were very valuable, and still are effective for many organizations, we realized the trend was toward more cerebral and less physical programs. Not everyone was comfortable with the outdoor activities, and that sometimes limited the primary purpose of the program—to strengthen the team. Fewer of our clients were choosing to utilize the adventure activities and the amount of time they were willing to devote to team processes was diminishing. Our staff still included one employee with specific expertise in the outdoor adventure component of team building, and at this juncture, he chose to form his own company specializing in outdoor and adventure programming. His departure left us with only one remaining employee—our administrative assistant.

Pat: Craig and I started to consider the advantages of establishing a home office. We were confident that we could handle our own administrative tasks, and most of our planning meetings and programs were either held at our clients' offices or at off-site locations. With only the two of us, a large home, and no kids, we made the decision to give up our office space and work at home. We had come full circle in fifteen years!

Our programming now ranged from working with small executive teams to leading interactive processes for large groups, some with more than one hundred participants. We purposefully didn't have off-the-shelf programs and designed each event specifically to meet the needs of that individual group. Clarity of goals and careful up-front planning were imperative, but Craig was also a master at seizing an unanticipated learning moment to enhance the value of the program. In fact, he was likely to change his approach in the midst of a program if he recognized a more effective way to accomplish a goal. That special ability to change horses in midstream saved him from misfortune more than once.

Craig: I was asked to give a lighthearted presentation for a sales organization that was honoring their top sales people of the year. I prepared an enjoyable and informative program around the theme of "Selling to All Types," confident that it would be fun and appeal to the entire sales force. I arrived at the venue with my one-hundred-plus handouts, energized and ready to go. While watching the scores of people file into the auditorium, I asked my host from what parts of the country all these salespeople had come. He said, "Oh, the only salespeople in attendance are the four who are being honored. Everyone else is from corporate headquarters, here to honor them." I had wrongly assumed that the sales force was honoring its

OWN top sellers. Here I was, standing in front of all these people, prepared to give a presentation that was totally inappropriate!

Fortunately, one of my strengths is the ability to adapt to change without panic. In fact, I rather thrive on the adrenaline. I was able to pull off the presentation as if I had prepared for weeks although I still regret that I had to throw away all those great handouts. Since that experience, I am much more careful about reviewing every detail with a client rather than relying on my own assumptions.

We had been using the MBTI, LPI, and several other instruments for years to help individuals and groups understand their own and other's strengths and operating styles. In the early 1990s, we also developed our own Team Assessment Survey (TAS) to help participants gauge how effectively they were working together. The TAS provides us with a wealth of information about the strengths of a team and the areas in which they need to develop and improve. With that knowledge, we can design the most effective team program possible. In addition to forced-choice questions, we included several narrative questions to gather more informal details about each team. The TAS helps give the team and its individual members a true investment in the program because it synthesizes their own data, and people trust their own data.

Pat: One question on the TAS that Craig added seemed a little off-the-wall to me, but it has provided some of our most valuable, interesting, and sometimes astounding information. That question asks respondents to name an animal that most closely resembles their team and to describe why they made that choice. Although some people leave it blank, most seem to enjoy the challenge. Descriptions range from "sneaky weasels," "scared mice," and "geese who blindly follow" to "constantly changing chameleons" and "skunks whose morale stinks."

While looking at the answers to this question presented by one administrative team, we realized that every single member of the team, except the manager, had listed their animal as a "trained monkey." We thought that was rather odd. In the midst of the team program, we asked the group why they all had chosen that animal and those exact words. Much to the chagrin of the manager, who was also a participant, the team members told us that he had described their jobs as so inconsequential that they could be performed by a trained monkey. So much for morale! We continued with the program, and at its conclusion had a lengthy discussion with that manager about mending the damage he had inflicted on his team. He offered a sincere apology to the group and changed the manner in which he interacted with team members. Eventually, they were able to move beyond that hurtful remark even though they never completely forgot about it.

Who would have guessed that a seemingly whimsical question would yield such insight? The answers not only provide clues for us as we plan a program but spark meaningful conversations among team members. The TAS has been a very effective tool for preprogram planning, and when readministered after a team building process, the responses clearly show what progress the team has made. We have implemented an Internet version of the TAS—one of the key components of our plans to start sharing our knowledge of team facilitation with other facilitators.

While most of our projects now fall under the category of team and leadership development, Craig also developed a partnering program for instances when multiple entities need to work together closely and effectively. Although the opportunities for delivering partnering programs have been limited, the results have been heartening.

Craig: I consider myself a facilitator rather than a trainer, and most of our programs focus on strengthening the team so its members can accomplish their goals as effectively as possible. One partnering program I facilitated included members of the military; federal, state, and local governments; construction organizations; and engineering firms. You can imagine all the different viewpoints, rules, and regulations that were involved in the joint project they were planning to implement. In a one-day program, everyone reached agreement on the goals, outcomes, and guiding principles they would follow throughout the project. They also agreed that if a problem arose, it would be resolved at the lowest possible level. I later received a call from one of the program participants who told me about a significant issue that had arisen. The team was able to solve it quickly without going up the chain of command. He estimated that they had saved three to six months of work stoppage by adhering to their agreement.

Throughout the years, we have always had as much work as we can handle without the need for formal marketing. Only once have we had a slowdown that really concerned us. That was when we decided to take a three-week vacation to Switzerland a few years ago. It was before cell phones were effective outside the United States, so we left a recorded message on our business phone indicating that we were out of the country and would return calls when we got back to the States. For almost two months following our return, business was very slow. We were getting concerned and made a concerted effort to contact former clients and get involved in even more community and business events than usual. Thankfully, the phones started ringing again.

Since that time, we have never taken an extended vacation, but other circumstances have impacted our visibility. Three years ago, we were contacted by a large health care organization in another city to work with several of their management teams. This organization was in acquisition mode and continued to engage our services with groups throughout the system. For a couple of years, that client accounted for almost 75 percent of our time and income. Once again, since we were spending so much time away from our home base, we had to make an extra effort to stay visible.

Contemplating the Future

We're currently involved with another large out-of-town project that limits our local participation for significant amounts of time. Due to this trend, and our fast-approaching senior status, we've done some serious thinking about our future. We have always advised our outplacement clients to find careers that fit their talents, experience, and *age*. We need to take that advice to heart in our own situation as well. It's hard for us to realize—and equally difficult for us to accept—that we're reaching the time when some people think of us as seniors. Now it's time for another adjustment to our business model—one of sharing our knowledge and experiences with others.

Craig: Program participants have started calling me "sir," and I look around to see to whom they are referring. Recently, after making a presentation to a health care organization, I was behind a couple of young women as we filed out of the room and realized they were discussing my presentation. One said to the other, "That was surprisingly good. When I saw that old guy up there, I thought for sure we were going to be bored to death." Much to my relief, she went on to say that her initial reaction was inaccurate and that she really enjoyed the program. However, her comments prompted some much-needed reflection. I related the story to Pat, and we began to seriously discuss what we consider to be another "morphing" of our business.

For the past several years, Craig has been doing executive coaching projects—a good fit for his level and length of experience. We're in the midst of adding a facilitator training component to our repertoire and have also developed a few products for facilitators, including an online version of the TAS. The old-guy comment just nudged us along in those pursuits. It also prompted us to start sharing some of the stories and lessons that we've learned throughout our journey.

Working with people and organizations is absolutely fascinating, and most of the time, it's enjoyable and rewarding. We have often ignored conventional wisdom and the rules of business. We have chosen projects that fit our strengths, our styles, and our comfort level. We have turned down business that wasn't well suited for our skills, and we have fired a few clients that were more trouble than they were worth. We still have plenty of energy and the commitment to help individuals and organizations do their best work. And, as long as we still have something of value to contribute, neither of us has any desire to retire.

Now that we've shared the chronological version of our journey, we'd like to tell you about our philosophy of doing business and share some of our most interesting experiences and observations. The following chapters are filled with stories—some humorous, some heartwarming, some serious, and some we'd rather forget. We hope you can gain insights from both our successes and our missteps.

CHAPTER 2

Know Your Strengths

Key determinants of long-term success are a person's awareness of natural strengths and aptitudes and the knowledge of how and when to apply those talents. Most people have never had (or have failed to take advantage of) the opportunity to determine what they do best. In the absence of that information, it's natural to take our own strengths for granted—assuming that if something is easy for us, it must be easy for everyone. Our years of experience in the field of career and leadership development and outplacement has upheld our belief that everyone has certain natural abilities, and the sooner a person determines what those are, the simpler it is to make important life choices. But we find that it is still the exception rather than the rule to meet individuals who have received comprehensive career guidance or have otherwise developed a clear picture of what they naturally do well.

Pat: As an alternative to the boredom of study hall, I worked for the guidance counselor when I was in high school. As in many high schools at that time, our guidance office was the place to go when you wanted to get out of class. We offered a couple of paper and pencil assessments and a stack of college handbooks, but little else. The key emphasis was on the decision of whether to go to college or not, and that was often dictated by family history, attitudes, and financial resources.

I knew I would go to college because that was a priority with my family. I took the only instrument available through our guidance office—the Kuder Preference Test. The results suggested I should pursue a career in social work, which held no appeal to me whatsoever. At that point in time, there was still plenty of gender bias surrounding career selection. I really wanted to be a lawyer like my father, but women were not encouraged to pursue such professions in the early '60s. Even my father discouraged that idea, reminding me that the only woman lawyer in our small town had never married, and he didn't want that to be my fate.

Still hoping the lawyer dream might some day become a reality, I majored in political science and enjoyed the course work immensely. Predictably, I married soon after graduation (as did more than half the women living in my section of the senior dorm) unprepared and unqualified for any specific career. I worked in the real estate section of a county government until my first child was born, and I became a stay-at-home mom. Eventually, I went back to school part time to earn a teaching certificate, and I was a permanent substitute teacher when I met Craig.

Craig's path was much different—he tried a little of everything! After a couple of college experiences—first at a residential and then a commuter college—he graduated with a degree in psychology. Like many young men in the midsixties, he looked toward the military as a first career step, attending Naval Officer Candidate School and serving two years in the navy, including a tour in Vietnam. When he left the navy, he tried many different jobs ranging from retail manager at a boatyard to stockbroker, kennel manager, public relations writer, salesperson for an extension university, and sailing instructor, just to name a few. Nothing held his attention for long, and these seemingly unrelated experiences didn't appear to point to any particular career path.

Craig: The only thing my numerous jobs had in common was that they were fairly short-term efforts, and I enjoyed them in the beginning but later found they had no appeal. I was worried, and a little embarrassed that I was apparently not mature enough to stick with any one thing. Tired of such a vagabond existence, I decided to go to graduate school where I completed a master's in counseling—a choice based on my enjoyment of working with people. I ended up taking a job as placement director at a university and moved to the Midwest.

When I arrived at the university, the department was a part-time placement office focused only on helping college seniors and graduates find employment. With little or no direction, I was charged with the task of developing a full-time operation. That fit my style perfectly—I love getting an enterprise set up and running. I was sure that a lot more could be done to help students decide what careers they might enjoy well before they were a few months from graduating. I wanted others to avoid the uncertainty I had experienced and was determined to offer career planning to students as early as their freshman year in addition to the usual placement services that most universities offered to seniors. I just wasn't sure how to make that happen.

While still in New York, I had done some research about the current state of the career planning field and discovered that the hottest book in the trade was Richard Bolles's **What Color Is Your Parachute?** *I read it but, quite frankly, found it only mildly interesting and put it on the shelf with my other books. Soon after arriving at the university, I attended a College Placement Association annual conference in Minnesota. It was informative, and I met lots of colleagues who were willing to share their ideas and expertise. The last breakout session I attended (after strongly considering leaving early for the airport) featured Richard Bolles. During that thirty-minute time period, my perception of myself and my career history was forever altered. It was truly a mind-changing experience and determined my lifelong vocation of helping others discover what they do well and love doing.*

I discovered that there IS a pattern in all my seemingly unrelated past jobs. That pattern involves figuring out how a system works and arranging the components for maximum potential. Once that is accomplished, my interest flags, and I'm ready to move on to the next challenge. While in the past I had considered my penchant for moving from one interest area to another to be a character flaw, I now understood that it was a gift. I also realized that my overriding skill—that of problem solver—could be applied to any number of career choices.

I figured if patterns could be identified in MY diverse past, they could be identified for anyone. This premise became the cornerstone of the philosophy and approach as I established the Department of Career Planning and Placement at the university. It also permeates all the professional development work I have done in our outplacement business and in our current work in team development and executive coaching. Pat and I both use the concept "do what you love" constantly in shaping and reshaping the focus of our business and our individual roles.

Helping other people discover their strengths and capitalize on them is the key to what our company has done throughout its existence. While Craig jokes that his ability to help others find a good career match comes from the fact that "he's tried them all," it actually comes from comprehensive career exploration—the most valuable service we offer to outplacement clients. Career exploration includes a battery of assessment instruments that help identify a person's interests, talents, learning style, leadership style, and much more. Most folks have literally "fallen into a job" or followed the path of least resistance in choosing a career. We soon found that, like so many others, very few of our outplacement clients enjoyed their jobs. But once they gained a clear picture of what they enjoyed and naturally did well, every one of them was able to let go of the past and become excited and confident about the future.

Pat: Mel is a perfect example. He was let go from a large manufacturing organization where he had been in the collections department. He had an imposing physical presence and a deep, booming voice—traits which had served him well in that role. But he admitted that while he was effective, he was not very happy with his job. In the course of taking the various assessments we used with our clients, Mel discovered that he was a global thinker. He liked to work with a whole system versus a small part of it. After finding out about his strengths and talents and completing an in-depth career exploration process, he chose to pursue a career in real estate development. He really enjoys being involved in a complex project from start to finish, drawing all the necessary people and resources together and seeing the final results of his efforts. He also enjoys being part of a team working toward a common goal as opposed to the combative role he had to play when working in collections. Years later, Mel's wife reports that he is excited to go to work every morning and is still energized at the end of the day. Stories like this one confirmed that the outcomes are well worth the mental and emotional effort we expend with our clients.

Discovering, and appropriately using, individual and group strengths is also a key component in the team building and professional development experiences we design. Most people think that they have to be adept at everything to be successful. We contend that no one is great at everything, and everyone is great at something. Discovering and concentrating on your strengths can help you avoid the pitfalls that Bob experienced.

Bob was the owner of the engineering firm where Pat worked for several years. During that time, the company grew from three to eleven employees. The staff members were young, energetic, and capable, and they possessed some very specialized state-of-the-art technical skills. Unfortunately, the owner thought he had to be involved in every function of the business rather than concentrating his efforts on his greatest talent—inventing.

Pat: Bob was a young engineer with several patents and an incredible gift for developing new technologies, but his management instincts left a lot to be desired. The director of engineering and I urged him to lock himself in a room with his drawing board and concentrate on his talent for innovation. But like many entrepreneurs, he felt the need to manage every detail, which led to several classic mistakes.

First of all, Bob hired relatives who were in need of jobs but were not necessarily suited for the available positions. Secondly, he rewarded a talented technician by promoting him to a management position. Unfortunately, the supervisory and administrative demands of management pulled the tech away from the hands-on work with the machinery that he enjoyed and did so well. The once even-tempered, easygoing tech became moody and difficult to work with. He also had little experience or interest in writing reports—a requirement of his new position. Most of his attempts had to be rewritten by others before they could be submitted to the contractors. In essence, we lost a great technician and ended up with an ineffective manager.

The company had numerous government contracts, which were gradually bleeding it dry. Payments were slow, and we consistently had to borrow on a line of credit to meet payroll. This was a time of incredibly high interest rates, so the debt kept growing. The one hope was to get a commercial product to market quickly. Bob demonstrated his brilliance once again by designing a lightweight protective suit for hazardous waste cleanup and firefighting efforts. There was definitely a need for the product, and we were able to locate investors and the venture capital necessary to keep the company afloat long enough to get the new product to market.

Pat: Predictably, the investors required that Bob concentrate on his design functions while they inserted their own professional management team to run the company. They also demanded a controlling interest in return for their investment. Our advisors urged Bob to consider the benefits of being part owner of a successful company versus sole owner of a dying concern, but Bob rejected the deal. Soon thereafter, the doors of a very promising enterprise closed forever. It was difficult to see the failure of a company with so much potential, and Craig and I vowed to avoid similar mistakes in our own business.

Having personally taken all of the assessment instruments we used with our career development and outplacement clients, the two of us were clear about our strengths and designed our roles in the company accordingly. We both really enjoy working with people and seeing them live up to their potential. Pat loves the organizational and detail work that keeps the company going on both a day-to-day and long-term basis. Craig has the talent and insight to identify what a person or an organization needs in order to thrive and is masterful at designing and delivering programs to meet those needs.

While Craig offers a big picture perspective, he is well aware that he isn't the best person to oversee the details, especially those relating to management and accounting functions. But in the earlier years when Pat had not yet joined the business full-time, he had to take care of some of those functions himself. Our accountant jokes that Craig practices "the circular theory of accounting"—meaning that when he isn't certain how or where to record an entry, he just circles it. We're not sure who was most pleased when Pat rejoined Career Resources—Craig or our accountant!

Strengths that are overused can also become liabilities. We have encountered many people who, like Bob, are sure they know the best way to do *everything* and are unwilling or unable to delegate responsibilities to others. We refer to such folks as "often wrong, but seldom uncertain." Mark fell into that category and proudly described himself as a take-charge guy. When we met, he was in his mid-fifties, president of a family-owned business, and beginning to prepare for his eventual retirement. He hired us to work with him and his management team, specifically to help him become more adept at handing over responsibilities to the other team members and to encourage the team members to step up and take charge.

In response to the request, we designed a two-day team building program with outdoor adventure components. Being in the construction trade, we knew the participants would learn best in an active hands-on setting. We had already conducted a personality inventory with this team, and to no one's surprise, Mark's results indicated he was an extroverted, take-charge, results-oriented person. Most of the other team members were more reserved and had become accustomed to carrying out Mark's orders rather than being proactive. As part of the team program, Craig devised an activity that would test Mark's willingness to give up some control and his ability to empower other team members to assume leadership responsibilities.

Craig: We started the program with a few easy warm-up activities. Then I challenged the team with a task called the Blind Square, which they were required to complete while blindfolded. I explained to the full team that

I would give them a piece of rope, and without anyone letting go of it, they were to create a square with the entire length of the rope while also determining the rope's approximate length. Mark took over immediately, directing the team as to how to proceed, but his initial idea didn't work. Undaunted, he was about to issue a second set of orders when, unbeknownst to the rest of the group, I pulled him aside and instructed him not to speak for the duration of the activity.

Usually during this exercise, people start talking all at once, throwing out ideas for solving the problem and arguing as to the best course of action. But this group was totally silent. The team members were waiting for directions from Mark! Mark was so uneasy with the silence he could hardly contain himself. He shifted his weight from foot to foot and sighed impatiently. The team had been well conditioned to delegate upward, and several minutes passed before they finally realized they would have to solve this task on their own. Once they realized that Mark was not available, they collaborated quite effectively to reach the goal. From that time forward, when Mark started to take charge at inappropriate times, the team reminded him about the Blind Square. The payoff down the road was that team members continued to engage in solving day-to-day business problems, giving Mark the opportunity to focus on more strategic issues as he prepared for his eventual retirement.

It takes time and patience to understand the strengths of people with styles very different than your own and to realize that your way may not always be the best or only way to accomplish a task. Something as simple as recalling an activity like the Blind Square can serve as a reminder to an individual or an entire work team until the learning becomes ingrained and creates behavioral change. Although the lesson of capitalizing on strengths can be accomplished through a symbolic activity, some people need more precise direction. Craig had the joy of helping one individual recognize his true strengths while observing the validity of the quote "We see the world not as *it is*, but as *we are*."

Craig: I was meeting with Ellen the vice president of a health care organization. From the assessment work I had done with her and her team, I was aware of their individual styles and operating preferences. Ellen was a "big picture" thinker who did her best work when she was given a broad goal without specific direction as to how to reach the goal or even a broad idea of what the successful end product would look like. In the midst of our meeting, her assistant Luke asked for a minute of her time to discuss a new project Ellen had assigned to him. I had the opportunity to observe their interaction.

This was before the days of computerized information storage, and Luke was in charge of maintaining all the records for the department. He was very conscientious and did his best work when he was given clear guidelines or could pattern a new project after a previous one. Ellen, in keeping with her preferred operating style, introduced the new project by saying, "We have a great opportunity here to do something really important. I'd like you to improve our records system!" Luke looked confused and asked her what she meant by "improve." Ellen replied, "You're the expert in charge of records. I want you to find ways to make our system better." When he asked again for more details, Ellen said, "I don't want to get in the way by giving you my ideas. Just use your creativity and make our records better." Hesitantly, the assistant backed out of the office, and Ellen and I continued our conversation.

About two minutes later, Luke interrupted once again to ask for additional clarification. "What exactly is it you want me to do?" he asked. She responded, "I want you to review our records system and make whatever changes you want in order to improve it." Luke left again only to return five minutes later to ask if it would be OK to reverse the alphabetical order of the records. By this time, both the VP and the assistant were beginning to exhibit signs of frustration.

After Luke left, I asked Ellen if she already had a vision as to what needed to be done to make the records better. As I suspected, she did but indicated that she didn't want to get in the way of Luke's creativity. I reminded her of Luke's operating preferences and suggested ways she might provide him with the information he needed without specifically instructing him as to how he should carry out the project. She called Luke back into the office and described a previous project, similar in scope to this one, which could serve as a model. She also shared some of her ideas and outlined measures of success for the project. Armed with this information and his past experience, Luke proceeded to do a magnificent job of revamping the entire records process and storage system in a way that far surpassed Ellen's initial concept.

This story is a perfect example of what can be accomplished when an individual is given the appropriate tools and the proper amount of direction to match his or her operating style. Our life's work has been to help others understand and manage their strengths and preferences. We gained that understanding firsthand through experiencing our own totally different styles. Our differences are especially evident when it comes to preparing for and delivering a presentation.

Pat: When faced with giving a presentation or facilitating a group process, I relate most to the Boy Scout motto—"Be prepared." I spend hours preparing and trying to anticipate all the issues and questions that might arise, along with determining the most appropriate way to address them. But Craig doesn't need to agonize or memorize in order to give a wonderful presentation. He just needs a general idea of the key points he wants to emphasize. Then he plays off the audience, the specific circumstances, and the surroundings as the presentation unfolds.

Craig told me well ahead of time that he was giving a presentation to a state teachers conference in Columbus on the morning of our first wedding anniversary. He prepared his handouts the day before and left early the next morning. About an hour later, he called to say he was on his way back to Dayton and asked if I would like to accompany him to Columbus that evening for dinner AND to listen to his presentation. He had arrived at the conference venue to find that he had overlooked one small detail—his presentation was scheduled for 7:30 p.m. rather than 7:30 a.m. While such an incident would have put me in a tizzy, it didn't faze Craig in the slightest.

I readily agreed to share a "rubber chicken" dinner for our anniversary, and late that afternoon, we headed to Columbus. We were about twenty minutes from the site of the event when he asked if I would jot down a few notes for him. I gasped and asked somewhat judgmentally, "Are you just now thinking about what you're going to say?" He answered that he had a pretty good idea of what he was going to cover, but he had just heard something on the radio that inspired him and that also tied several of his key points together perfectly. I was stunned that he didn't have a written and memorized presentation since that would have been the only way I would approach the situation. I was also slightly apprehensive about being present for what I feared might be a less than stellar performance in front of 150 people! On the contrary, the presentation was compelling and wonderfully received. I have to admit that since then I have always been proud—and a little bit envious—of his presentation skills.

Craig: If I have to follow a written script, I bore myself, not to mention the audience. This is especially true if I have to read a prepared presentation. I need inspiration, and I draw my strength from playing off the energy of the audience. On one occasion early in our partnership, Pat and I were asked to give a joint presentation to a professional association. I was especially busy, so Pat took the lead in designing the presentation and producing the visuals (overheads were state of the art at that point in time) with fairly limited input from me. Being a very visual person, she prepared an overhead for every point we wanted to make, which also served as her security blanket. I found that to be especially confining as my usual style of presentation is free flowing and based on audience reaction and participation. But, in this instance, I felt the need to stick to the script so I wouldn't throw Pat off her agenda. As a result, the presentation was uninspiring to say the least. I just about put myself to sleep!

We learned our lesson from that experience and decided there were ways we could capitalize on our different approaches and presentation styles. We found that our opposing strengths gave us a huge advantage in working with groups just as it did in working with individuals in the outplacement phase of our business. We developed a very effective presentation that introduces the elements of personality type from each of our very different perspectives. Observing us in action makes it particularly easy for participants to determine which style is most similar to theirs, and they are able to identify their own preferences more accurately. Our presentations are full of humor with the ultimate message being how advantageous it is to work with—rather than against—someone whose preferences are different than your own. Individuals end up identifying with one or the other of us, depending on their own preferences. And people are constantly amazed that we are able to work so well together given our extreme differences!

The word began to spread that our programs were both enjoyable and valuable, and we were contacted to facilitate a major team development program for an international hospitality organization. We determined after meeting with the general manager that it would be important for the team members to begin the process with a greater understanding of their own individual strengths. We had been advised by the GM that there was one participant who was very resistant to anything he perceived to be a touchy-feely exercise. He added that, while Aaron was absolutely fantastic at the technical part of his job, his relationship skills were very weak. Aaron was considered by the others to be arrogant, abrupt, and unpredictable.

Craig: During the beginning of the program, as we introduced the strength awareness part of the process, Aaron's body language exuded negativity and contempt. He was obviously daring us to show him anything he didn't already know. After listening to us describe and tell stories about different strengths and operating styles, his interest began to grow. When I described his style as being the same as many TOPGUN pilots, his skepticism turned to excitement, and he began sharing his profile with others around him. Every person in the room was amazed by the change in Aaron's attitude and behavior.

On the second day of the process, we explored how individual strengths might play out and be used to the best advantage as well as what the blind spots and downsides might be. Surprisingly, Aaron seemed relieved to understand the potential negative applications of his style and began to see how his behavior might be difficult for others to understand and tolerate. As a result of this understanding, Aaron accepted our suggestion to enroll in some professional development courses focused specifically on people skills. We saw him several months later at a reception and were absolutely stunned at his transformation. He was engaging, attentive, and absolutely charming. In addition, he seemed delighted with his newfound interpersonal skills. According to his manager, who was wonderfully surprised at Aaron's 180 degrees turnaround, Aaron would not have lasted much longer in his job had he failed to adjust his attitude.

One of Craig's greatest strengths is his problem solving ability. His success comes from his tenacity and resourcefulness. He simply won't give up until he has solved the problem or exhausted every avenue imaginable. Those traits are invaluable when working with individuals and groups, and they were especially helpful to our outplacement clients. When one avenue didn't work out, Craig had ten more options that the person could pursue.

Pat: I also benefit personally from Craig's problem solving abilities and perseverance. I was in the midst of a very busy week which included facilitating two separate leadership programs. After a full-day program in Dayton on Thursday, I was to leave early Friday for a two-day Leadership Ohio program elsewhere in the state. Wednesday evening, I gathered the things I would need to pack for my trip while doing some laundry. Included in the laundry was a shirt that had a map of the state of Ohio embroidered on it. Joan, a participant in the Leadership Ohio program, had just given me that great gift, and I intended to wear it during the upcoming program. Much to my horror, when I pulled it out of the washing machine, I saw that the embroidered colors had bled onto the rest of the white shirt. I tried several products to take out the stains, but nothing worked.

The ruined shirt was in the back of my mind throughout the following day. I couldn't think of any other means of getting rid of the stain, and even if I did come up with a solution, I didn't have time to implement it. I was quite upset, knowing that Joan would be disappointed that I didn't wear her gift. I returned home that evening to find the shirt on the bed, carefully folded, without a hint of the offensive stains. I knew Craig was responsible but couldn't imagine how he managed to pull off such a miracle. I was even more amazed at his explanation.

Craig: I also had a program to facilitate on Thursday, and it was scheduled to end in the early afternoon. I had been thinking about how to solve the problem of Pat's shirt, and the only thing that came to mind was OxiClean—a new product that was advertised on television constantly! We didn't have any, and at that time, it wasn't sold in stores; it had to be ordered. During a break, while talking with some folks who were attending my program, I mentioned the dilemma and asked if anyone knew where I could get some OxiClean. One program participant said that he had some at home, and he lived nearby the training facility. He went to his house during the lunch break and brought back the magic potion. I hurried home after my program, OxiClean in hand and washed and dried the shirt. By the time Pat arrived, the shirt was sparkling white.

Pat: Craig's perseverance saved the day! He was definitely a hero in my eyes. I was also grateful to the person attending his program who went out of his way to help. In retrospect, we probably should have written to the manufacturer of OxiClean with that testimonial. We might even have been offered a lifetime supply!

In addition to knowing their strengths, people need to be aware of the fact that those strengths may not always be valued by others. In his days at Wright State, through a long and circuitous process, Craig ended up in a conversation with an international health-related organization about the possibility of helping them develop a career planning process for people who were forced to change careers due to health issues. He was excited to learn he was being considered to head up the project. The position played into some of his key strengths— developing a new and potentially groundbreaking program, setting up a process to help people make the most of their strengths, and, as the resident expert, having a key role in the development process. He went into the meeting with Dr. Leonard, the chair of the organization, with high hopes.

Craig: One thing we always taught in our job interviewing courses was how to ask questions to obtain insight into an interviewer's perspective on a potential job. People can use the same words yet have a very different picture of how things might play out. Prior to this interview, I felt I had clearly established my credentials for the project and fully expected to be offered the job on the spot.

After some preliminary small talk, I asked Dr. Leonard how he saw this project unfolding. He said that the first step would be to appoint an MD to head up the project. I was a bit stunned and inquired why it was necessary to have an MD. Dr. Leonard talked about the need for credibility in the organization in order to get funding for the project. Still assuming I would be the one in charge, I inquired if the MD's role was that of a figurehead. He responded that the MD would be responsible for the project, not me.

This made no sense. I had already established a successful university department using a similar process and assumed an MD would not have the interest or the expertise in setting up such a program. But it also became obvious during our discussion that, without the MD title, this group would consider me a "second class" citizen. While I don't need power or accolades, I do require the freedom and flexibility to make decisions. It was clear from Dr. Leonard's responses that I would have neither.

Despite this red flag, I pursued the issue a bit further. The chair informed me that he thought project planning would take a couple of years—to study career planning systems that currently existed and then to develop their own process. I reiterated that I had recently completed a very similar process for the university and felt that, with a few minor modifications, we could use that as a model and be up and running almost immediately. He considered my comments for a moment and then repeated his previous statement. His meaning was clear. My past work and potential contributions would not be utilized or valued, and if I accepted a job with the organization, I would have limited impact. Since I am most effective in situations where I can make tangible contributions and bring value, his comments destroyed my interest in the project. I thanked him for his time and left. To my knowledge, this very important project has never been implemented.

Craig understood when to walk away from an opportunity that might potentially make him miserable. Even though the content was a great fit for his knowledge and interests, the mechanics of how he would be required to operate were in opposition to his preferred style. Many people accept employment because they CAN do the job; they neglect to determine whether they WANT to do the job according to the stated requirements.

A book entitled *Do What You Love, The Money Will Follow*, written by Dr. Marsha Sinetar, was quite popular in the late '80s. It captures the essence of what we believe about career and job choices. First, take the time to determine the essential components of what you are good at doing, what you most enjoy, and how you prefer to do it. Then find an occupation that incorporates as many of those components as possible in your day-to-day job activities. Using your strengths is much more energizing and rewarding than spending time doing things counter to your preferences. The enjoyment we've experienced over the past twenty-five-plus years in business proves the validity of that concept.

Things you can do to discover your strengths

- Ask your parents or siblings what you spent your time doing as a child. Usually, the same kinds of activities will hold your interest throughout your lifetime.
- Ask your spouse, family, and/or friends what seems to energize you most.
- Think about your current and past jobs. Determine what dimensions of those jobs are/were most pleasing. Think about *how* you like to operate when you're doing your best work as well as *what* activities you like to perform.
- Look for recurring patterns in your jobs, education, and leisure activities.
- Take some assessments like the MBTI, LPI, etc. to determine your strengths. Several are described in the appendix.
- Work with a career coach or executive coach.
- If you already know your strengths and what you love to do, try to incorporate more of those activities and talents into your current career.
- If you dislike what you do, start looking for a career or job that will make the best use of your talents.

CHAPTER 3

Value Differences

One of Craig's favorite sayings is, "Differences aren't good or bad, they're just different." Appreciating differences in others is just as important as knowing and using your own strengths. Two heads are better than one, especially if they bring substantially different points of view. Our combination of differences—plus the fact that each of us almost always values the input of the other—is a key factor in the success of our business. We've saved each other from mistakes more than once by offering a different perspective or filling in pieces of information the other has missed. But, from time to time we still find ourselves forgetting our own words of wisdom even in the midst of discussing the topic of differences.

Pat: Craig and I were planning a presentation for the Dayton Rotary Club. The meeting was on Valentine's Day, and the person in charge of scheduling speakers thought it would be fun to hear from a married couple that also works together. We entitled our presentation "Celebrate Your Differences" but lost sight of the concept as we started to plan for the event.

Before we began to design the presentation, we each prepared by doing some research. I did an Internet search, and Craig read a book of jokes—typical of our different approaches to life in general. Then we sat down to discuss our ideas. I had my pen and notebook in hand and was ready to get down to the specifics of putting our thoughts in outline form. Craig started with a suggestion that sounded great, and I wrote it down. We discussed the concept in a bit more detail and I was off and running with that theme, convinced that we were making great progress in record time. Even as my pen was poised in midair, ready to record the next step in what I thought was a logical progression, Craig piped up with a second approach—totally different from the first! I responded rather sharply that I thought we had just agreed on a concept and asked why he was always changing his mind. Craig said he thought it was clear that we were brainstorming possibilities and asked why I always tried to put things in sequence and come to closure before we had considered all the options. We paused, took a few deep breaths, and broke out laughing! We realized that our conversation was a classic display of our differences in action. The fact that the disagreement occurred while planning a talk about "celebrating differences" made it all the more humorous. We decided that the story would be and ideal opening for our Rotary presentation, and it brought many appreciative laughs from the audience.

Since we view the world so differently, we have a whole repertoire of those kinds of stories and use them liberally when working with teams. We learned early in our life together to appreciate our different perspectives and use them to our advantage, but found that many people we work with in business settings are convinced that they must have the right answer at all times. It's very difficult to persuade some folks that there may be several right answers and more than one way to achieve a desired result.

Craig: The manager of the loan department at a local bank asked me to help him with a personnel problem. Jeff was frustrated with two individuals in his department. Their jobs were identical and included marketing and handling all the paperwork involved with initiating loans. I asked him to explain the problem. According to Jeff, one of the men really enjoyed the outside sales components of his job, meeting new people and talking about all the services the bank could provide, but he disliked the accompanying paperwork he had to complete back at the office. Consequently, he always had a huge backlog, and what was completed was often done in a sloppy manner. The other employee was great at getting his paperwork completed, and it was always done accurately, but he was reluctant to get out of the office, network, and meet new people. Consequently, he didn't bring in much new business. Jeff wanted me to work with both of the employees to help each one develop the skills he was lacking.

As I listened to his story, I didn't perceive that Jeff had a problem at all. I suggested that he divide the job responsibilities according to each person's strengths. One could be the outside person responsible for bringing in new business. The other could be the inside person who processed all of the paperwork generated by his coworker. It made perfect sense, would be easy to implement, and would cost nothing! Jeff was unable or unwilling to grasp the concept. He maintained that the job description was fine and that he just needed to find two people who could perform all the required functions. After investing a great deal of money on motivational and time management programs, trying to develop each person's weaknesses, he ended up firing both of the employees and searching for two new people. I'm not sure how the new hires worked out, but I know it would have been easier and less expensive to adjust the job requirements to match the skills already demonstrated by the two experienced employees.

A similar story of valuing differences had a much more productive outcome. Craig worked with the director of a department at a large hospital system to help her enhance her delegation skills. She was especially frustrated with one of her reports who had a very different operating style than hers. Maggie was very precise and linear in her thinking and tended to micromanage her staff. Ethan was especially unhappy with that approach.

Craig: I discussed different work styles with Maggie and urged her to give Ethan a project with clear expectations and a specific deadline and then to back out of the picture. Although apprehensive, she gave Ethan an important project to complete. At the end of the following week, she passed him in the hall and casually asked how the project was going. Ethan enthusiastically replied that he had just completed section six. Maggie was delighted. The entire project consisted of nine sections, and she had estimated that it would take about five weeks to complete. After just one week, Ethan had completed two-thirds of the project!

The second week ended, and Maggie let her curiosity get the best of her. She asked, once again, how the project was going. Based on Ethan's earlier progress, her expectations were high. He enthusiastically replied that he was currently working on section two. Maggie's brow furrowed as she asked how he could possibly be on section two when he had completed section six a week earlier. Ethan replied that he had worked on one part of section eight, moved on to section two, and planned to tackle section five later in the week.

Maggie called me in a panic. It was beyond her comprehension as to why anyone would work on portions of a project out of sequence. I explained that some individuals were global thinkers and didn't necessarily proceed in the step-by-step manner that she preferred. I urged her to let Ethan complete the project using his own approach and reminded her that the only thing she needed to be concerned with was the final product and the fact that he met the agreed-upon deadline. She accepted my advice, and Ethan completed the project to her satisfaction in the expected time frame. Maggie shared with me that she and Ethan had developed a much better understanding of each other's styles and how they complemented each other. Months later, they were still laughing about the famous project!

We are extremely thankful for our different styles and talents when it comes to the many interesting circumstances we encounter in our consulting work. Between the two of us, we have most of the bases covered. We were presented with a particularly challenging situation while working with the executive team of a food franchise. One of the executive team members had been a participant in another of our programs in her previous job, and she persuaded the two owners of the franchise that they really needed a team retreat.

Marge and the other managers were experiencing several issues that prevented them from performing at a level that would help the organization to thrive. The team had completed the TAS, and the results revealed several key problems that impacted them—conflicting directions from the two owners, the frequent absence of one of the owners, and an overall lack of long-term planning or direction for the company. The survey indicated that the team members—minus the owners—worked well together. But the tension was taking a toll on the rest of the leadership team.

The retreat started out quite positively. The team had completed a personality style inventory in addition to the TAS, and the processing of that information was very enlightening for them. Many of the team members had never been exposed to an operating style instrument and were eager to learn the implications of their individual and collective profiles. They had a good balance of "detail oriented" and "big picture" team members, and each person seemed to understand and value the talents of the others. It soon became evident, however, that there was a major stumbling block to the smooth operation of the organization. What held the team back and created a huge drain on its time, energy, and resources was the combative relationship that had developed between the two owners. Marge was assertive enough to put that issue on the table just before the lunch break.

Marge met with us during lunch to explain the situation as she saw it. The original owner, Sam, was in his early sixties and close to retirement. A few years earlier, he had handpicked Arnie, a man in his late thirties, to become an equal partner with the goal of handing over management of the company to him upon Sam's retirement. Sam considered Arnie the son he never had and was eager to teach him and nurture him every step of the way as he looked forward to the time he could hand over the reins. But things hadn't progressed as Sam had envisioned.

In addition to generational issues, Sam and Arnie were opposite in almost every imaginable way. Sam was an empathizer, nurturer, and teacher with the very strong personal values of his era. Arnie was brash, dictatorial, and convinced that he was always right. To make matters worse, Arnie had had an affair with an employee even though he was married. That behavior was counter to every moral standard that Sam embraced, and the relationship between the two began to crumble.

Pat: So here we were in the middle of a team building process when this information was dumped in our laps. When we gathered after lunch, the room was completely silent as everyone waited to see how we would handle this situation. Craig and I had huddled for a few minutes to decide how to salvage the rest of the program in a way that would prove beneficial to the team and the organization. We formulated a plan based on our very different styles and talents and shared it with the team. The program had been scheduled at a state park with lots of beautiful green space with the intention of conducting some outdoor activities in the afternoon if that seemed appropriate. So Craig took the team—minus the owners—outside for team experiences that would both enhance their ability to work together and allow them to relieve some of the tension they were experiencing. I stayed in the training room with Sam and Arnie in an attempt to help them break their stalemate. The owners pledged to the team as they left the meeting room that there would be some kind of resolution to their issues by the time they returned.

For the first thirty minutes, Sam and Arnie sat with arms folded, facing in opposite directions, and refused to speak directly to each other. One would speak to me, demanding that I convey the message to the other even though they were seated a few feet apart. It was a flashback to the days of dealing with our children when they were very young. I continued to reiterate that they had promised their team to resolve this intolerable situation. I warned that if their efforts failed, it was likely that there would not be a company left for either one of them and no jobs for their employees. We still weren't making much progress until I mentioned an attorney I knew who specialized in conflict resolution. I suggested that, at the very least, they could agree to meet with her and see where that might lead. That was the solution that they presented when the team returned. It had taken three hours to get them to agree to that one item! The team accepted the solution and pledged to hold the owners' feet to the fire.

On our way home after the retreat, I told Craig how glad I was that I didn't have to be outside with the team conducting activities and leading discussions for three hours. That just isn't my strength. Craig laughed and said he was equally as happy that he didn't have to sit in that room and try to convince Sam and Arnie to come to some kind of resolution of their differences. Once again, we had demonstrated the undeniable advantages of being partners with different styles and preferences.

We still had doubts that Sam and Arnie would make good on their promise. But when we followed up with them a couple of months later, we learned that they had met with the attorney, and eventually, they agreed to part ways. The attorney helped them reach an agreement for Arnie to buy out Sam's interest in the company. Sam retired, the company survived, and a number of jobs were saved.

How much we have learned over the years from situations like that one! It's amazing to observe the differences in the way people operate—more often than not without any sense of how their behavior impacts others. Craig is a master at setting up scenarios, such as the one described next, that bring people to that realization. As mentioned earlier, Craig has facilitated Leadership Dayton's opening retreat for many years. Each year brings another group of forty community leaders together, who were eager to share their approaches, interests, talents, and differences. At one of those retreats, Craig led an activity called the Domino Man, which revealed how differently people can approach the same problem.

The class was divided into four groups based on their different operating styles. Each group was challenged to construct an exact replica of a figure Craig had built, using the entire contents of a box of dominoes. Every like-numbered domino had to be placed in the exact location as in the model in order for a team to successfully complete the task. Teams could plan as long as they liked, but once they began construction, they were timed to see how long it took to complete the challenge. While Craig didn't indicate that it was a contest, the mere fact that it was timed made all the groups assume they should work as quickly as possible.

Craig: The construction phase was chaotic as people ran back and forth from their work tables to the model. There was talking and shouting among team members as they tried to get each domino in the correct position as quickly as possible. Throughout all of this action, I noticed Stan standing back a bit from his team, just observing the action. When the challenge was completed, I led a discussion about the different ways they completed the process, what the reasoning was behind each approach, and how well each group thought their team had performed. There were several comments about how they all assumed it was a race simply because the process was timed. Stan didn't say anything during the discussion about his actions, and I chose not to single him out.

Later that evening, Stan approached me and wanted to talk about some insights the activity had provided for him. I asked him to explain how he had performed the task. He said he had studied the puzzle carefully and had put his three dominoes down on the outline first—in precisely the correct positions—and then stepped back and watched. At that point, he considered his work to be done and decided to get out of the way of the others.

Months later, Stan talked to Craig about the activity once again, saying it had been a great eye-opener for him. He was a partner in a professional firm and explained that he now realized why some of his fellow partners and staff got provoked with him when they were working on a big project that required coming to the office on a weekend. Stan's approach was to come in very early before the others arrived. He would complete his part of the project, leave his contribution on the work table with a note, and go off to play golf. He truly thought he was carrying his share of the load. But after the Domino Man activity, he started to understand why some people at work accused him of not being a team player. After considering the circumstances, he decided to adjust his behavior to the needs of the team and spend more time interacting directly with them on future projects.

Organizations typically spend little time determining whether the physical work structure suits the different preferences of the individuals who work within it. We remember when the open-office configuration was first instituted in one of Dayton's large corporate headquarters. While some people thrived on the interaction, it was very distracting to others who needed a quieter environment to do their best work. Those preferences came into play during a program Craig facilitated for a call center group where the employees' sole responsibility was to answer questions from people calling for information about transportation schedules. During the program, the participants complained about their working conditions, and Craig led a discussion to find out what the specific issues were and to help them determine some creative ways of making their jobs more interesting and less stressful.

Craig: Each person was assigned to a cubicle in a large open room. One thing that became clear during the discussion was that some members of the team were more introverted than others, and they were especially bothered by the noise level when everyone was talking at once. They reported that the more extroverted people not only talked louder on their calls, but also chatted with other team members when they were not involved with a customer. This was very distracting to the employees who had a preference for a quieter work environment. After brainstorming some ideas of how to improve the situation, the team decided to rearrange the office. I asked the group to form a line ranging from the person with the greatest noise tolerance to the one with the greatest need for quiet. Then they exchanged cubicles. The person with the greatest need for quiet moved to the back of the room. The others took the cubicles in order and the person with the highest noise tolerance took the first cubicle in the front of the room. This simple cost-free solution accommodated people's differences, enhanced productivity, and, according to an employee survey, led to greater satisfaction.

The differences between people with a preference for introversion and those with a preference for extroversion are profound and fairly easy to recognize. In the Myers-Briggs Type Indicator (MBTI), those terms refer to the amount of energy a person derives from interaction with the world around them. When we were facilitating a career development program with the employees of a plant in rural Nebraska, we found that a majority of folks there considered themselves to be introverts. Many were farmers who also worked a shift at the manufacturing plant, and they were very comfortable living in this quiet rural setting. One glaring exception was a man who was participating in the corporate management training program. As a requirement for that program, he was being rotated to each of the plants throughout the country and would eventually end up at corporate headquarters. He was clearly extroverted as indicated by his behavior as well as his score on the MBTI. He was also from New York City where he was accustomed to lots of noise and activity. It was readily evident that he was having a very difficult time in this extremely small rural environment. In the course of a conversation, he told us that he would periodically become so desperate for interaction that he would drive to the one stop sign in town and sit there until another car appeared just so he could wave at the person in the other car! Needless to say, he was elated when his four-month tour of duty ended, and he could head back to a more populated area.

It's interesting how extroverts find ways of dealing with introverted environments. A young woman at the same plant also needed more interaction with people than her work situation afforded her. She worked in the accounting department, and her office space was one of a group of about fifteen cubicles in a large room. Unlike the call center described earlier in the chapter, this room—primarily populated with introverts—was extremely quiet for hours at a time. This extrovert could cope only so long each day before she sought interaction with others. Occasionally, she would even start tossing paper wads over the walls of her cubicle until someone responded and began a conversation with her.

Pat: Craig and I are both extroverted and can easily relate to both of these individuals and their desire for interaction. When Craig leaves on a trip, I always have a list of things in the office and the house that I'm determined to accomplish while he's gone. Invariably, within a few hours of his departure, I'm on the phone talking to friends and setting up lunches and other activities that will give me the chance for interaction in his absence.

In most other ways, especially those defined by the MBTI, Craig and I differ dramatically. Craig is much more empathetic than I am—very attuned to the feelings of others. While I consider myself very approachable, I don't immediately relate or connect with everyone I meet like Craig does. Another of my primary motivators is the desire to save money or get something for free. So, when we're on vacation, I always look through the magazines that have information about events, amusements, and restaurants in search of coupons for free stuff. On one trip, I talked Craig into going with me to look at a time-share. In return for taking the tour, we would receive a coupon for a free dinner at an excellent restaurant.

Pete was our salesperson, and Craig immediately struck up a lively conversation with him. Pete was quite creative considering the time-share condos had not even been constructed yet. Undaunted, he showed us all the layouts and architectural drawings for the planned development and then drove us to the construction site to point out what a wonderful view "our condo" would offer when it was completed. Pete was entertaining, and we actually had an enjoyable time. When we got back to the sales office, Pete sat us down at a table, brought us coffee, and disappeared into the back room obviously to gather the papers we would need to sign to be become satisfied time-share owners! Craig got a very concerned look on his face and said, "I really like Pete, and he's going to feel so bad when we tell him we don't want to buy a time-share after he spent so much time with us." I explained that I liked Pete too but not enough to spend thousands of dollars on something that we didn't want! Needless to say, I took responsibility for telling Pete the bad news and requesting our dinner coupon. After we were in the car, I reminded Craig that probably 99 percent of the people who take the tour do it only for the dinner coupon! Craig continued to feel bad for Pete while I considered the ability to deal with rejection to be part of his job description.

Another huge difference between the two of us is Pat's need for structure and Craig's desire for what we call "wiggle room." This difference played out when we were reunited at the airport after Pat had been to a week-long training seminar for the administrative managers of the public accounting firm where she worked at the time.

Craig: Pat walked into the terminal with a huge grin on her face that I assumed was meant for me, but that was only partially true. She proceeded to tell me she had had a life-changing experience during her week away. I love hearing about life-changing experiences, so I was awaiting the story with high expectations. She dug into her brief case and pulled out a large leather day planner. This was back in the days when such monstrosities were first being introduced, so I wasn't immediately familiar with what it was. I certainly couldn't understand, by any stretch of my imagination, how this notebook could have changed her life. She then launched into an animated description of how the day planner made everything so much more efficient—she could write something in one place and make reference to it somewhere else and on and on until I'm sure my eyes glazed over. I simply couldn't imagine owning a calendar that required me to go to school to learn how to utilize it.

Pat: I saw immediately that Craig was not particularly interested in my day planner epiphany though he was trying very hard to share my enthusiasm. It seems we have very different opinions about what constitutes a life-changing experience. To my way of thinking, he needed the day planner much more than I did! His definition of a filing system is to have ten piles of file folders stacked on the floor around his desk. His explanation is that he really has trouble filing things because he can think of four or five topic areas for each folder. And, if he files something away, he totally forgets about it and can't find it when he needs it. With his "floor filing" system, he keeps running into important information, and thereby things get accomplished much more efficiently. Despite this appearance of disorganization, he always seems to know how to locate the information he needs. When I request something and he says, "Look in the fourth file in the second pile from the right," that's usually exactly where it is! So we agreed to each utilize the system that works best for us.

Years after my day-planner experience, Craig tried using a similar product. But he used it just like he used his small pocket calendar. It seemed rather foolish to drag around a three-pound day planner when he could accomplish his needs with something much smaller. It was just one more lesson in understanding and appreciating our differences.

We eventually decided that it's not only important to understand differences, but also to learn how to make adjustments when the situation requires it. We not only had to manage our own very different operating styles, we also had to accommodate differences with other team members. Pat prefers things scheduled down to the minute while Craig and a third member of our team building program staff approached projects in a "free form" manner. This presented a special challenge as we prepared for a very important project—one of our earlier team building programs. The event involved managers from a large international corporation with participants from all over the world. They worked on the same large account via telephone and e-mail, but most had never met. The main goals of the program were for the participants to get to know each other as more than just a voice on the phone, to enhance the feeling of belonging to a team, and to have fun in the process.

We used an operating style inventory so the participants could understand their own and each others' preferences to accomplish more effective communication. The venue was a state park, and we planned a number of problem solving activities, both indoors and out, plus four specific outdoor challenges to enhance teamwork among the participants that would carry over to their interactions on the project. Each of our staff of three—plus an additional trainer from one of the local challenge courses—was in charge of facilitating one of the outdoor challenges. Participants were divided into four groups, and each group rotated through the four activities. We planned to spend thirty-five minutes to complete and process an activity, plus ten minutes for participants to regroup and proceed to their next location.

Pat: It was no surprise to anyone that my major concern was timing. I knew I would absolutely stick to the schedule in order to accommodate the timing and the design of the program and that Craig and the outside facilitator would as well. But our employee, Dan, was reluctant to be tied to any time frame. He argued that experiential programming shouldn't be subject to strict schedules because it's impossible to predict how long a group will take and how thoroughly they will want to discuss their experience. While I understood that premise and Dan's preference for a more fluid time frame and discussion period, this situation was an exception. If one group arrived at their next activity and had to stand there for fifteen minutes waiting their turn, it would upset the entire progression of the program. It was extremely critical to have everything run with precision for a program and group of this size. After some heated discussions, Craig joined me in insisting that this was one time when we ALL had to adhere to a very precise time schedule regardless of our different preferences. Everything went as planned, and I think even Dan agreed that the trade-off was worth the end result.

We get annoyed with the pundits who attribute all differences to gender. As one can see by many of our stories, that premise certainly doesn't hold true for us. Craig was the one who felt bad for Pete because we weren't buying a time-share. Pat is the one who enjoys the financial and legal aspects of the business. Pat is an avid football fan while Craig is a music lover. Differences come from many influences. Our goal is to help people find out what they truly enjoy and translate that into a career, job, or hobby that takes full advantage of the person's talents, interests, and passions.

We get lots of enjoyment out of watching people demonstrate differences when they don't even realize what they are doing. Craig worked with a group that included the president of an organization and the managers of each of the branch offices in the region. The president was a "big picture" person, and the managers, without exception, were very detail oriented. That's logical. The managers deal with day-to-day operational realities while the president is responsible for the future direction of the organization. The way those differences were demonstrated during the program was classic.

Craig: The group was discussing how they could capture the best practices of each office while cross-training and sharing knowledge and information among themselves despite the geographic separation. The team was struggling to come up with solutions when, suddenly, the president jumped up out of his chair in a state of great excitement. He grabbed three or four markers and began drawing grand swirling figures in different colors with multiple lines of intersection—it could have been a work of modern art. He said, "There, that's how we can do it" and sat down with a huge grin on his face, waiting for the others to comment on his idea. There was total silence as everyone puzzled over the figure. The president was crushed that no one else could see what seemed perfectly clear to him. We talked about the incident and finally came up with specific useful suggestions that flowed out of his grand concept. It was a perfect example of how the president often introduced new concepts and didn't understand why they weren't immediately embraced by the managers. After that program, he concentrated on presenting his ideas in a more concrete manner.

We have observed that people have different opinions and diverging philosophies on almost everything—even how to mow grass. Craig worked with two separate organizations that had overlapping responsibility for maintaining green space areas in the community. They were in conflict about whether or not the grass should be mowed and, if mowed, what length it should be. One organization's primary focus was preserving wildlife, and therefore they objected to mowing the grass at all. The second organization focused on recreational use of open space, and they wanted neatly trimmed areas for people to play games, hike, picnic, and enjoy nature. After lengthy debate and discussion, each group gained an understanding of the other's motives, and the two organizations agreed on ways to settle this issue and future disagreements. This serves as another example of how simply discussing differences—whether they are inherent tendencies, ingrained personality traits, or philosophical disparities—often leads to understanding, agreement, and positive outcomes.

Things you can do to value differences

- Assess your blind spots—what might you be missing?
- Be open to differing realities and seek to understand how others view the world.
- Don't assume that because someone operates differently than you do, they are deliberately trying to aggravate you.
- When making important decisions, seek the input of someone with a different perspective than yours. Your differing styles can be quite valuable to each other.
- Read a book or subscribe to a magazine that has a subject or focus very different than your usual interests.
- Attend seminars and discussion groups that deal with subjects that you don't normally explore.

CHAPTER 4

Every Silver Lining Has a Cloud

While most of our recollections center around positive experiences and successful projects, as in every organization, we have had some unpleasant times when things just didn't work out the way we had planned. Thankfully, we've had only a few such instances considering the many years we've been in business, the hundreds of programs we've delivered, and the large variety of organizations we've served. But the comfort of many successes doesn't erase the vivid memories of our more difficult encounters. Hopefully, our experiences can alert others to possible pitfalls. At the very least, hearing about our experiences may help you realize that no matter how carefully you plan, when you're working with groups of people, the outcome cannot be scripted.

In the early years, while our business was primarily outplacement, the main problems we encountered were the result of individuals who were upset—sometimes rightly so—about the way they had been treated by their former employers. Usually, that anger took the form of a verbal tirade that was soon forgotten once the client started focusing on the future. However, we did have some uncomfortable incidences, two of which were somewhat frightening.

Craig: We were informed by a client company that they were terminating one of their employees, and I went to their offices to meet her. I always tried to meet with a new outplacement client as soon as possible so I could explain our services, give encouragement, and provide suggestions about how to cope with breaking the news to friends and family members. As I arrived at the company's human resource office, I learned that the woman was being informed about her job dismissal in the adjoining room. A few minutes later, a corporate security officer arrived to warn me that the woman was known to carry a gun in her purse and to assure me that he would be nearby if I encountered any problems. I must admit I was apprehensive as I entered the room to meet her. I'm not sure what I would have done if she had reached into her purse! Fortunately, our conversation went smoothly, and my heart rate gradually returned to normal.

The second incident took place at an outplacement center that was actually located within the corporate headquarters building of a company undergoing a significant multiyear downsizing process. We had strongly advised against putting that outplacement center on-site as we knew it was very difficult for individuals to return each day to the place where they no longer worked. To make matters worse, the space occupied by the center was a huge glassed-in area on the first floor of corporate headquarters. It was essentially a "fish bowl" where folks could be observed by their former coworkers or anyone else entering the building.

Pat: One day, I was discussing the services we offered at the center with a newly outplaced individual. He was quite distraught about losing his job, and in the course of our conversation, he mentioned that he was a gun collector and owned quite a large stash of weapons. He went on to say, "Maybe I should just bring my collection here and show it to those people upstairs," referring to the executive offices on the top floor of the building. I took a couple of deep breaths while I searched for an appropriate response. I said something to the effect that, while I assumed he was joking, he wouldn't be doing himself any favors by discussing weapons or by referring to any type of retaliation.

Although we maintain the strictest confidence when working with clients, this was obviously an exception. After he left the center, I shared his comments with corporate human resources and security. The following day, several corporate officials spoke with the individual who indicated that his comments were in jest. He decided not to come back to the job center, but the company assigned a security officer to the area for several days just in case. It took me a couple of weeks to get over the uneasy feeling I experienced each morning on the way to work.

A third incident posed no serious threat except perhaps to our sanity. A vice president at a large healthcare organization was extremely angry that he had been dismissed from his job. The organization claimed that it was strictly a financial decision and initially gave him 6 months of severance pay and unlimited outplacement services.

Craig: We fully understand how difficult it is to experience job loss and were used to dealing with all types of reactions from our clients. Usually, new clients spent anywhere from a few days to a few weeks working through several emotional stages. We prided ourselves on our ability to help people see their situation as an opportunity rather than a tragedy and to get them focused on the many new avenues that were now open to them. Despite our efforts with James, he held on to his anger for months. He spent lots of time and energy attempting to get back at his organization. His behavior actually had a much greater impact on us—the very people who were trying to help him—than it had on his former employer.

After the first several months, it became obvious that this was not a typical situation. James spent hours each day talking—often long distance—to anyone who would listen about how he had been wronged. Our phone bill skyrocketed! He also conducted these conversations with his feet up on the mahogany desk, waving his full coffee cup in the air as he talked. After he left his office each evening, we applied scratch cover to his desk and attempted to clean the stains on the carpet. Finally, out of sheer desperation, we presented him his very own *sealed* coffee mug.

Craig: James refused to take our advice to narrow his job search to a particular geographic region despite the fact that such a strategy was proven to shorten the search process. In fact he ignored most of our advice, not in a nasty way, but rather in a passive-aggressive manner. We kept thinking that he would begin to take his job search more seriously as he drew closer to the end of his severance package. At the beginning of the final week of his six-month agreement, James entered my office with the news that he had negotiated with his former employer for an additional few months of severance.

Our concern was primarily for James since it was clear that he was having difficulty putting his past behind him. We knew from his behavior over the first six months, that he was more intent at getting back at his former employer than getting on with his life. A second concern was for the employer. The company had declared the termination to be financially driven, so the longer the organization continued to provide full pay and benefits to James, the more they would be at risk if he decided to sue for wrongful dismissal. And finally, we were bearing considerable expense, both financial and emotional, supporting an individual who was not serious about getting on with his life.

Craig: Eventually, I met with the vice president of human resources at James's former place of employment. After discussing the risks to everyone involved if the severance package were to remain open ended, he decided to set a final and nonnegotiable end to the severance benefits. At that point, James became more serious about his job search, and several months later—slightly more than one year after we began working with him—James accepted a job offer. Apparently experiencing some feelings of guilt for his behavior, James told his former employer that we deserved a larger fee for our extended efforts. The company offered more, but we turned them down, preferring to honor the fixed fee we had originally agreed upon.

Some companies used outplacement services only to ease their guilt, and once in a while, that approach came back to haunt them. One company consulted us in December about a major downsizing but refused to follow our advice to wait until after the holidays to make their cuts. They ended up dismissing their entire accounting department without realizing they wouldn't have anyone left to carry out their year-end accounting functions, including processing payroll and year-end bonuses for top management. When they approached a few accounting employees to come back on a temporary basis, all of them refused. The company had to hire people from a temporary agency to accomplish the necessary tasks, and the process did not proceed smoothly.

When we added team building to our business services, there were different kinds of risks involved. Obviously while conducting outdoor experiential programs, including challenge courses, the liability risk was a concern. After a couple of years, we discontinued using the high ropes component and chose to develop program activities that achieved the same goals without the potential risks. We were fortunate that, throughout our many years of experiential programming, the only injury sustained was a sprained ankle. In the years after we stopped using high ropes courses, we have heard several stories of serious injuries and even the death of an individual who was participating in a high ropes course program.

As anyone in the people business can readily attest, there are times when things don't go according to plan. For the most part, our problems and missteps have been mild. We learned a few lessons from them and continued on a bit wiser. But one incident still gives us both sweaty palms just thinking about it.

Pat: Interestingly enough, the same company that provided us with one of our most positive experiences also contributed the program that still raises our heart rates at its very mention. It was a terrific company with a dynamic and enthusiastic group of managers. We had designed and conducted several programs for them, including a one-day teamwork program with their sales service management group. That group rated our program more highly than the Getting to Yes seminar, which was hugely popular at the time. So we were absolutely delighted to be asked to work with the company's entire sales organization—a group of almost one hundred people from all parts of the country.

The sales group scheduled a week-long program at a large hotel, and we were asked to develop a fun, lighthearted event for a couple of hours at the end of their final meeting day. They asked us to plan something active since attendees would be spending much of their week in meetings and training sessions. We knew the organization tended to hire young male athletes, taking advantage of their highly competitive spirit by rewarding those who could sell the most products. What we didn't know was *how* competitive they were, the extent to which they would be cooped up and confined during the week of the seminar, and a couple of other details that turned out to be quite significant to the outcome.

We met with the vice president of sales well in advance and presented our ideas for the event. Our plan was to divide the group into eight small groups and have them rotate through eight different problem solving activities. Each group would receive points for completing the activity correctly, and everyone would celebrate successes together at the end of the event. The goal was to focus on enhancing their problem solving skills and sense of camaraderie and to provide an enjoyable ending to their week-long meeting. Our proposal was warmly received and we looked forward to the day with anticipation.

Craig: We arrived at the hotel several hours before the program to set up the activities, each in different breakout rooms, which surrounded a large meeting room. Everything was ready well before the 4:00 p.m. start time, and we eagerly awaited the arrival of the participants. The first sign of trouble was an auditory one. You could hear the group coming down the halls of the hotel, marching and chanting, "Boom! Chugalugalug, Boom! Chugalugalug!" Then they appeared—two women and eighty-four men all under the age of thirty-five. We soon realized that the vice president had neglected to tell us a few important details: the number of hours participants had been sitting through classroom-style presentations; that the company had introduced our session as a "battle of the teams" and had provided different color jerseys for each team; and, most disturbing of all, that the participants were arriving from a prolonged open bar happy hour.

Pat: As we observed the participants entering the room, we began to fear the worst, and that is exactly what we got. No one paid much attention to Craig as he attempted to explain the activities and goals for the event. He stressed that this was NOT a competition but rather a fun event designed to promote and take advantage of their problem solving skills. We assigned the groups to their respective activities and then watched in horror as they transformed the problem solving experiences into contact sports. Group members from one team were dispatched to sabotage the efforts of other teams, and young men were literally hurling their bodies at each other to prevent a rival group from completing an activity. The two women were huddled in a corner!

The vice president refused to intervene, and, after a couple of light fixtures were broken, and two people were injured (one taken to the emergency room), we turned off all the lights, closed the doors to the activity rooms, and ended the program. It was a complete and total disaster. We tried to get a meeting with the vice president a few days later to discuss what had happened and why and, of course, to apologize for any part we may have played in triggering the mayhem. Unfortunately, our calls were never returned. We ended up paying for hotel damages out of our fee and were never able to acquire any work with that company again.

It's easier to accept such a debacle if there is a lesson to be learned from it, but try as we might, we have never come up with a lesson from that experience. We felt we had been diligent in asking questions and designing an appropriate program for the event as it was described to us. We had no way of knowing the participants would be drinking liberally before the session. In hindsight, perhaps the only thing we might have done differently was to "turn out the lights" at the first sign of rowdiness. Fortunately, we have never again encountered anything even close to that experience!

The more knowledge we gained, the more we learned about the right questions to ask when planning a program. Sometimes company leaders aren't always aware of potential issues, or if they are, they ignore them and don't share them with the consultants. That's what happened when we were contracted to develop a program, train trainers, and help facilitate a corporate "learning experience" for a Fortune 500 company.

This organization had a history of embracing each new business fad. They had "flown with the buffalo," installed a mammoth granite boulder in their lobby during the "move the rock" popularity, and preached (not necessarily practiced) the *Seven Habits of Highly Effective People*. We had worked with the organization several times and were asked to assist them in designing and facilitating a day-long learning session for all five-hundred-plus employees at their corporate headquarters. The theme was, "Encouraging the Heart," and they were using materials from the Leadership Practices Inventory developed by James Kouzes and Barry Posner. The key message was to acknowledge employees who made worthwhile contributions and to encourage people to speak up and offer ideas for improvement. We were asked to design the agenda and materials for breakout sessions and train leaders for each breakout group. Each of us would also lead a group.

After several meetings, it was decided that, during the breakout sessions, small groups of twelve to fifteen people would brainstorm ideas and suggest ways the company could encourage engagement and input from all employees. At the end of the breakout sessions, we would meet with the president and VP of human resources to integrate the information gathered from all the groups into four or five specific ideas to be adopted throughout the organization. These ideas were to be presented by the president to the entire gathering at the end of the day.

Craig: We felt the program was well designed and looked forward to the event. Pat really enjoyed preparing the materials, and I liked training the breakout session leaders. We had several meetings with the president and HR vice president and were impressed by their commitment to involve everyone in the organization and encourage employees to share their ideas.

The breakout sessions went well, and the groups generated many useful ideas. At the end of the breakout sessions, the employees gathered for a presentation in the auditorium. Meanwhile, we met with the president and HR vice president to combine the data gathered from the breakout groups and to prepare the president for sharing the results with the employees at the conclusion of their presentation.

Craig: The data was quite clear. Employees were excited to have the opportunity to be more candid, receive and provide more feedback, and gain recognition for their ideas and contributions. However, when we presented the data, the two executives were not particularly receptive. The HR vice president said to the president, "Well, this might be what they said, but here's what they really mean" and proceeded to change the data to reflect what he and the president had predetermined to present to the employees. Pat and I fought hard to get them to understand what a terrible mistake they were making. We cautioned them that when the employees realized their input was being totally disregarded, they would be extremely reluctant to offer ideas in the future. It was all the more damaging since the theme for the entire learning day was to "encourage the heart"! Our advice fell on deaf ears, and the president stood before five hundred employees and presented his own data while claiming it was produced by the employees. He fooled no one, and you could literally feel the energy and enthusiasm drain out of the participants like air escaping from a balloon. Pat and I were as disheartened as the employees were.

Over the years, we did quite a bit more work with that organization. However, it was only after both the president and human resources vice president had been replaced! The atmosphere by then was decidedly different and a much better match for our style of programming.

We've always been very trustful of the people and organizations we meet and work with, and that trust has almost always been well founded. However, in the case of one potential client, we were duped not once, but twice before we figured out what was happening. We had targeted this particular company as an organization we would like to add to our client list, so we were delighted to receive a call from the human resource director requesting that we submit a proposal for an in-depth program to help employees prepare for, and make the most of, their retirement. We were told that there was some urgency to implement this program, and the proposal was due within a week. We dropped other projects to meet the deadline.

We got very creative and developed an individualized program that covered three areas: how to spend time productively, how to enhance and maintain health, and how to maintain financial well-being. We consulted other experts for the financial and health components while we concentrated on the segment that would help participants determine what would really bring them satisfaction—hobbies, volunteer work, or even starting a small business. We brought our team together and worked long hours to complete the proposal in the time requested. In our eyes, the final product was something of a masterpiece, and we anxiously anticipated a reaction from the company. When we could wait no longer, we called to find out if a decision had been made and were told that, while they really liked the proposal, they had decided against implementing it. We were disappointed, of course, but hoped we might get another chance with this company in the future.

Sure enough, about six months later, we received another call from the human resources director. This time, he requested a proposal for a career development program for company employees to help them determine appropriate career paths. We had been doing a similar program for another company for a couple of years, and it was much easier to develop this proposal and meet another short deadline. We submitted the second proposal quite confident that it would be accepted since we had so much experience doing exactly what the company was requesting. We were a bit shocked when our proposal was rejected.

Soon after the second rejection, we happened to be talking with a former employee of that same company. In the course of that conversation, we discovered that the company had implemented both programs we had proposed in precisely the same format that we had suggested. They had used their own employees to deliver the programs! Older and wiser, the third time the HR director requested a proposal—this time for a team building program—we replied that we would be happy to comply, but there would be an up-front fee for the proposal, which could be applied to the cost of the program if they decided to proceed. The request was withdrawn. We did facilitate several team building programs with that company in the ensuing years, but it was always at the request of department managers. We sidestepped the human resource director.

While management can be difficult, so can employees—although we find that their behavior often reflects the way they are treated by their organization. Craig was asked to work with a company's information technology department that reportedly was having some internal strife. The department head was convinced that his employees were difficult people and took no responsibility himself for any of the problems. He decided his team needed help and sent them off to a one-day team development program, refusing to participate himself.

Craig understood that the program would probably be challenging given the department director's refusal to participate, and he designed the agenda to take that into consideration. Unfortunately, Craig's mother passed away two weeks before the program date. He decided to proceed as scheduled, but he was still feeling the sadness of that loss very deeply. Of course, he did not share this personal information with the group or their manager.

Craig: As the program participants began filling the room, I noticed that there was very little talking or interaction among them, which is pretty unusual. Before we got started, I attempted some small talk with a few individuals and got very little response. I started the morning by asking the participants what they would like to accomplish, thinking that would get them talking, not just to me but to each other. My question was met with stony silence. Some of the folks were people I had worked with before in very successful programs, so I was truly surprised and confused by their behavior.

I moved on, introducing the agenda and asking if it would meet their needs or whether there was anything they would like to add or eliminate. What little response I got was rude and negative. I really wasn't in an emotional state to exhibit my usual patience, so I paused and asked the group to tell me what was going on. Finally, one person shared that their boss had told them they "were a bunch of misfits," and he was sending them off "to be fixed." They had decided among themselves to attend the program but to refuse to participate.

I acknowledged the validity of their reasons for not wanting to be there and said they were welcome to leave, or they could determine among themselves what they wanted to accomplish during the day, and I would do my best to make that happen. Once they had vented their anger, they all decided to stay. I helped them use elements of the MBTI to determine the best ways to work with their customers, which seemed to be a helpful tool for them. At the end of the day, the group indicated that it had been time well spent.

That day taught me an important lesson. There is no way of knowing what personal or workplace issues may be affecting a group or an individual on any particular day. I had always felt personally responsible for ensuring that every program participant had a breakthrough experience. Now I realized that, for any number of reasons, I might not be able to positively affect each person in each group no matter how hard I tried. That was my own breakthrough, and since then I tend to put a little less pressure on myself.

As time went on and we encountered more and more unexpected situations, we learned that sometimes the people who hire us have their own hidden agendas. Or sometimes they are just completely clueless as to what is really going on in their organizations. Occasionally, the deck is stacked against us for a particular program or event. One of those difficult situations surfaced when Craig was asked to facilitate a business planning retreat for the partners of a professional firm. He worked with the partner in charge to design the agenda, which included activities and discussions to encourage the partners to work together more effectively and perform as a team.

While Craig was asked to direct most of the retreat, the partner in charge inserted one agenda item that he would lead himself. That item was listed as a discussion of the firm's pro bono work and wasn't explained in any further detail. As it turned out, the discussion was a personal and rather vicious attack on one partner who dedicated much of his time—supposedly at the direction of the partnership—to pro bono work. The other partners accused him of not pulling his weight and not bringing in enough paying clients. Coming late in the agenda, the negativity of that segment nullified most of the progress gained from earlier team building activities and discussions. It was apparent to me that the partner in charge had orchestrated a group attack based on his reluctance to talk to this individual on his own.

After being blindsided a few times by the personal agendas of company executives and team leaders, we saw even more value in using our Team Assessment Survey as a basis for designing customized programs. We began suggesting that organizations include the survey as part of the team process. This instrument gives us input from each member of a team, not just from the manager or team leader. Also, since the survey data is generated by the team members themselves, it gives them a keener sense of ownership in the improvement process. As we have learned, people trust their own data. With a greater awareness of the strengths and needs of the team, we are in a stronger position to help them accomplish more in a shorter period of time.

Even with the use of the TAS, we don't always have the impact we hope to have. We were asked to work with a small manufacturing business owned and operated by a husband and wife. In addition to the owners, the management team included seven others. We used a personality style assessment and our TAS to gather information. After analyzing that data and meeting with the owners, we designed a program that included a two-day, off-site session and several follow-up meetings—some with the owners alone and some that included the management team.

Pat: I was particularly excited about this project because the husband and wife had very different styles and personality profiles. Craig and I had been so successful learning to take advantage of our differences that I was confident that we could help Alex and Joanne do the same. They even had profiles that were similar to ours. Joanne was extremely organized, a sequential thinker who wanted things to be planned and under control at all times—preferably under HER control. Alex was an idea generator who thrived on change and didn't like to be tied to any process or set of procedures. Unlike Craig and me, they neglected to work things out together before dealing with their management team or their general employees. The TAS clearly indicated that the managers were confused and constantly received conflicting information from the owners. Either owner was apt to rescind or change a directive or request issued by the other, creating constant upheaval. I was still hopeful that once the owners and their team understood each others' strengths and preferences, they would be able to work out their differences for the benefit of the company.

We took the owners and management team off-site for a two-day retreat. Day one included processing the personality inventory including experiential activities to demonstrate similarities and differences and a discussion of what each person had to offer to the team. On the second day, we focused on the results of the TAS and the issues the survey raised. The group also discussed the advantages and challenges of working for a family-owned business and, more specifically, how the communication styles of the two owners impacted the rest of the team.

The owners were both extroverts and tended to air their personal and professional disagreements with the team members, who were mostly introverted. That not only made the team members uncomfortable, but the conflicting information they received was very confusing. Since the managers couldn't determine whose directions to follow, either nothing was accomplished or a decision was made that was later reversed.

During the retreat, the team gained a great deal of understanding about each other and about the owners from the assessment information, activities, and discussions. They were able to voice their frustrations and request solutions to the problems that they constantly encountered due to the owners' styles and behaviors. Some clear goals were established, and Joanne and Alex pledged to try to work through plans and projects together before presenting them to the rest of the team. We felt the whole team had developed a good basis of understanding that would relieve a lot of tension and conflict going forward.

Craig: We did several follow-up sessions with this team after the retreat and saw quite a bit of improvement in how they operated. Mainly, now that the team understood the conflicts between the owners, the managers made more decisions among themselves and worked more closely with each other. However, a few years later, the owners' relationship, coupled with the results of some fraudulent activities committed by a former employee, led to the demise of the company.

These difficult programs, although small in number, forced us (albeit reluctantly) to accept the fact that we can't win them all. Both of us take our real and perceived failures very hard, but we have finally gotten used to the fact that some companies don't want to accept our advice even when they seek it, and that's beyond our control.

Things you can do to avoid the "clouds"

- Get to know your client—the more you know, the fewer surprises you'll encounter.
- Deal with the highest level person you can and ask *lots* of questions throughout the planning process.
- Develop a detailed work plan and have your client sign off on it.
- Be prepared for the unexpected and determine how you can diffuse situations if they occur.
- Accept the fact that you won't be able to please all people all of the time—no matter what you do.
- If things go wrong, analyze what happened and determine how to avoid that in the future. Discuss your observations with the client and get their reactions.
- Then forgive yourself and try to forget.

1979—One of our first pictures together, shortly before we were married. We started our business a few months later with $300 and two promises: 1) never to put any more of our own money into the business and 2) never to borrow any money. We have kept those promises to this day.

Mid 1980's—We're scoring occupational assessments for a career development program in Nebraska. A manufacturer contracted with us to design, develop and facilitate programs for employees throughout their organization. Over a ten year period we worked with executives, managers and office staff as well as the folks on the manufacturing lines. It was a very worthwhile and satisfying project.

Late 1980's—Craig and fellow Board members of the Dayton Chamber's community leadership program trying out the "low ropes" challenges at an outdoor recreational center. This was the beginning of our venture into team building and outdoor adventure programming for corporate teams and not-for-profit organizations.

Early 1990's—Craig observes a group during an outdoor team retreat. This activity, called "spider web" reinforces trust, teamwork and safety. Craig is ensuring that the group is keeping everyone safe and observing the group process in order to lead a discussion about the lessons participants learned from the activity.

1991—Pat in one of our three offices. This was during the height of the outplacement frenzy and our company occupied a suite of offices in downtown Dayton while maintaining two satellite offices in nearby communities. Maintaining these offices as well as conducting team retreats and career development, programs around the country was a challenge.

1991—For this project we designed and facilitated two-day team building programs for three different groups of 60 participants each—180 participants in all. The participants all worked on one huge project in locations throughout the U.S. and Europe. It was fun and rewarding—and we facilitators were exhausted and exhilarated by the end of the week.

1992—Another of our very favorite programs was held at a remote rustic camp in Colorado at an altitude of 10,000 feet. Even though it was April, we had enough foresight to rent a 4-wheel drive vehicle. Here Craig is ready for the trek up the mountain. The car made it over a frozen stream bed and all the way to the top. Some of our participants weren't so lucky and had to carry their luggage for the final mile.

1994—By this point in time Pat had become more comfortable with the outdoor adventure programs we facilitated. She even climbed to the top of the imposing 30 foot high "pamper pole" which was strategically placed overlooking a deep ravine.

1997—By 1997 we had sold the outplacement business and the two of us were running our consulting firm from a home office. The children were out of the nest and we decided to reward ourselves with our first real trip—3 weeks in Switzerland. Since cell phone coverage wasn't reliable overseas, we left a voice mail message explaining that we would return calls when we were back in the States. We were surprised to find that it took almost 3 months to "jump-start" our business again. "Out of sight out of mind" proved true in this situation.

2002—Pat planned and facilitated the program days for the Dayton Chamber's Leadership Program for 10 years. This picture was taken at Wright Patterson Air Force Base which has a significant positive impact on the Dayton area. The aircraft in the picture served as Air Force One during the Kennedy administration, and was the plane that carried Lyndon Johnson and Jacqueline Kennedy back to Washington after President Kennedy's assassination.

2002—Participants in a community leadership opening retreat are enjoying activities that help them get acquainted and learn to work as a team. Over their 10 month program, they discuss issues and hear from experts in such areas as education, economic development, arts and social services. Many remain actively involved in the community as a result of their experience. The Rider Group facilitates retreats for leadership programs throughout the country.

2006—Despite the fact that we still run the business full-time, Craig occasionally gets the chance to engage in his passion for sailing. Before moving to the Midwest, he was in the boating business and an avid sailor. He participated in numerous competitions, including the Trans Atlantic race from Bermuda to Denmark.

CHAPTER 5

Savor the Magic Moments

While the horror stories are hard to forget, they are far outnumbered by good and great experiences. For us, magic moments are measured by the breakthroughs our clients achieve. Our individual career development and outplacement clients provided us with many opportunities to celebrate. When those clients turned the corner and began to view their job loss as an opportunity, we knew they were on their way to a positive future. We were fortunate enough to share those moments of joy and optimism with each person as he or she moved on to a new job or made a successful career change.

In some cases, group programs also yield individual success stories as in the case of this father-son breakthrough. We conducted a program for teens and their parents at the request of our church's youth minister. After experiencing one of our Myers-Briggs programs, he asked us to work with a group of families to enhance the appreciation for the gifts of individual family members. The goal was to demonstrate how MBTI differences can explain some of the challenges families face in valuing and relating to each other.

Prior to the program, we administered and scored the MBTI instrument for each participant. During the group program, we explained the four elements that make up the MBTI, using activities to help them experience firsthand how different preferences are exhibited in behaviors. After each person determined a "best fit" type, we reconvened the family groups to discuss individual styles and to talk about how their preferences might explain the relational dynamics they were experiencing. We then asked them to answer questions about how they could use this knowledge to value each family member and make their relationships more rewarding for all.

Craig: The conversations between family members were lively and focused. After they discussed their questions in family groups, we asked for participants to share their insights. Several families related that the MBTI information gave them a better appreciation for each other and a basis for more positive family interactions. Finally, one father stood to speak. He was employed by the military, and his personality type is one that views the world in terms of right or wrong and doesn't hesitate to make his opinions known. He was very emotional despite the fact that public displays are uncommon for his type. After regaining his composure, he described new insights about himself and, more importantly, a new appreciation for his son who was his exact opposite in MBTI terms. He said, "I want to publicly apologize to my son for all the years I made him feel like there was something wrong with him. I now appreciate who he is and love him very much for being that wonderful person instead of the person I thought he ought to be." There wasn't a dry eye in the room as the father and son embraced.

Another wonderful individual discovery occurred as we conducted a career development program for a small privately owned corporation. Pat worked with an administrative assistant who was unhappy in her current job and concerned about her future.

Pat: Jean, a woman in her thirties, was a "floating" administrative assistant. She was a single mother and was very discouraged with the combination of pressures at home and an uninspiring job. She expressed a desire to be in sales, and when she mentioned it to the human resources director, he suggested that she should leave the company and work in a department store for a while to acquire some sales experience. That just wasn't an option—financially or psychologically.

During my discussions with Jean, she mentioned that she had researched the issue and had concluded that her company should appoint retail liaisons to interact with the retailers who carried their products. Many of the stores were small family-owned businesses, and their owners didn't fully understand the benefits of the product or the best ways to set up their displays. The liaisons would advise the stores as to how to place, display, and advertise products to optimize sales, which would benefit both the company and the individual stores. A sales liaison position was Jean's dream job.

We knew that the president/CEO of this company was very open to new ideas and willing to listen to his employees regardless of their place in the company hierarchy. We also knew that the company was at a point where it needed to boost product sales. I worked with Jean to help her develop a proposal explaining the advantages of creating a sales liaison position and coached her on presenting her concept to the president. As a result of her presentation, Jean was named as the company's first sales liaison and was given six months to prove that her idea could bring value to the company. She did just that and was the catalyst for the company hiring several additional liaisons. We saw Jean a couple of years later, and she had transformed from a tired, uninspired employee to a stylish, enthusiastic, and confident professional.

Helping individuals reach their potential was a large part of what we accomplished during our years in outplacement. When we began working with teams, we discovered that it's a much greater challenge to orchestrate a magical experience for a group of ten, twenty, or fifty people. Although it's difficult to inspire everyone at the same time, we have been fortunate to play a role in numerous epiphanies, when groups have gained the insight necessary to change the way they approach or perform some aspect of their business. Those are the magical moments that consultants and facilitators truly savor and replay in their minds when they need inspiration.

Craig: Soon after we started working with teams, while attending advanced training in the use of the MBTI, I helped members of an organization achieve a significant breakthrough in the way they related to each other. As part of the workshop experience, I partnered with another class member for an actual group intervention. We decided to work with a social service agency to gain more experience in that realm. To start the process, we interviewed Mary, the agency director, about the current group dynamics of her staff and what she hoped our intervention would accomplish. She reported that there was tension among her staff, especially between the counselors and the financial/government reporting staff. Mary wanted people to have a better understanding and appreciation for each other's contributions. We decided to use the MBTI as a tool to talk about valuing differences.

The combination of the individual MBTI types represented by the agency gave us a good idea about what was causing the tension. Mary was a visionary and her style was very appropriate for her position in the organization. The majority of the service providers were "change agents," and they were well suited to work with clients to help them make positive life changes. The three reporting and finance people, the "stabilizers," were focused on administrative details and government regulations as required by their positions. According to Mary, everyone else in the agency treated the stabilizers with great disdain, claiming they made life miserable by constantly demanding information for reporting purposes.

Craig: During a half-day program, we reviewed the fundamentals of the MBTI with the agency participants and led a discussion about differences. The change agents referred to the stabilizers as "those darn data people" and insisted that constant demands for reporting information put a damper on their creativity and enthusiasm. Rather than lecture about the importance of each role within the agency, I decided to ask questions to get them to reflect on the reality of the situation. How does the agency get funding for its mission? What are the reporting requirements necessary to continue to receive that funding? Who makes sure that all the reporting requirements are met in an accurate and timely manner? What would happen to funding if the information was not submitted to the government in a timely manner? Finally I asked, "What would happen if there weren't any stabilizers to take care of all those requirements?"

Suddenly, the rest of the group realized how very valuable the "darn data people" were to the agency. The agency couldn't exist without them. In breakout groups, they discussed ways they could all work together more effectively and how the required data and information could be collected more efficiently. By the end of the program, the change agents were thanking the stabilizers for their valuable contribution. They finally realized that all types were valuable and necessary for the overall functioning of the organization.

A major team development project came our way when we were contacted to design and facilitate the quarterly meeting of the executive team of a large manufacturing company. The team included the corporate officers and the presidents of each of their subsidiary companies—fourteen individuals in all. To this day, we don't have to think twice when asked to recall the most successful and enjoyable program of our career. That was IT! Had we realized at

the time what an enormous impact that program would have on the direction
our business would take, we probably would have been too frightened to pull
it off the way we did.

*Craig: Jack, the human resources director who contracted with us, was
a nervous sort. He was new in his position and the responsibility for
the entire three-day meeting of all the corporate officers had him on
edge. He hadn't worked with us before and had no idea what to expect.
Like Pat, he was most comfortable in situations where the events were
carefully scripted. Pat and I met with him to discuss goals and objectives
and to develop the agenda. It was determined that we would design and
facilitate two of the three program days, after which the participants
would have a third day to discuss their internal business. Jack initially
suggested the business meeting should take place the first day, but I
recommended putting the team component first. Later, the participants
marveled at how much they accomplished in their business meeting due
to the understanding they gained during the previous two days of team
development.*

The location was a rather rustic camp in a remote area. The meeting facility
was a cozy lodge. The nearby sleeping accommodations were small log cabins
with iron cots. The camp had both high and low ropes courses that could be
incorporated into the program as we saw fit. While we had used experiential
programming for some leadership programs, we were quite careful about when
and how we used ropes courses. In this case, it was an excellent choice. The
company manufactured adventure and outdoor equipment, and the officers
were a young and, with one exception, all-male group with a penchant for
taking on physical challenges.

*Pat: Jack arrived at the camp early the morning of the program kickoff
to make sure everything was in order and to deliver food and drinks to
supplement the simple camp fare that would be provided. He was extremely
nervous and, upon leaving, reminded us that "things HAD to go well." His
comments and demeanor didn't do a lot to soothe our own apprehensions
as we went about setting up the room for the morning's activities.*

*The sound of tires on gravel, shouting, and laughter announced the
arrival of the participants. Even before they reached the door, it was easy
to tell they were a lively and outgoing group. I wondered if we would we
be able to command their attention to accomplish the program goals, but*

my fears proved unfounded. While the group was jovial and eager to have a good time, they were also intent on success and learning.

The morning was a combination of cerebral and experiential. We used a personality style inventory plus several group activities designed to demonstrate the importance of understanding, utilizing, and taking advantage of the strengths and differences of the team members. The materials and concepts were well received, and the members of this group threw themselves wholeheartedly into every activity and discussion. After several hours of interactive indoor programming and group discussions, we headed outside to utilize the camp facilities for experiential activities that would cement the morning's formal learning. This part of the program used Craig's abilities to full advantage as he set up challenges that emphasized issues the group needed to explore.

Craig: You never know what is going to happen during an outdoor experiential program, which is part of the appeal for me. I selected challenges that I thought would highlight dynamics relevant to the team and prepared to take advantage of learning opportunities whenever they presented themselves. In this program, everyone participated fully and persevered with each challenge that was presented until they had solved it to their liking. The CEO set the tone. He obviously considered himself on the same level as every other team member. He never expected, requested, or accepted any special treatment, and it was very obvious that he had the total respect of each team member which he returned in spades.

As a predominantly extroverted team, the biggest issue was their need to *really* listen to each other. We noticed that individuals were often thinking about what they were going to say when they got the chance to talk rather than listening to what others were saying at the moment. So we decided to present them with a challenge that would require them to deal with the art of listening.

Islands is an activity that involves getting a team to move everyone from one island (a small wooden platform) to another and finally on to a third. The only resources are two wooden planks, neither of which can span the entire gap between the islands. In the process of accomplishing the task, no individual and neither of the boards can touch the ground. If anyone steps off an island, there are consequences as determined by the facilitator.

Craig: Because of the competitive group dynamics and their issue with listening, I decided to put everyone on the same island to start since doing so would magnify these tendencies. As a result, they were densely packed and literally on top of one another. True to their usual pattern, they dove into the challenge with great enthusiasm. By design, not everyone could effectively see the actual problem or the resources that were available to them, but this didn't stop anyone from voicing strong opinions about how to proceed. In the process of struggling to see what was happening, one of the team members stepped off the island. To highlight the team's failure to comprehend how each person's actions impacted the others, I informed them that the penalty was blindfolding one of the team members. Even though the individual would no longer see what was happening, he still had to participate in the activity just like everyone else.

When I chose Bernie to wear the blindfold, he demanded to know why since he had "done nothing wrong." I explained that one individual's actions impact all members of a true team. Bernie was the corporate attorney, and I chose him for several reasons. First, while participating in the other activities, he had not actively contributed when we discussed the outcomes. Second, since he was positioned away from the main action area, he didn't have a clear picture of the task, the resources, or what was involved in actually solving the problem. These circumstances resembled his actual role and relationship to the team at work and gave him a very different perspective than other team members.

In the course of successfully solving the challenge, the team decided to walk Bernie across the plank first. After they placed him on the second island, he was largely ignored by the rest of the team. Occasional updates were offered, but he wasn't included in conversations or consulted about potential solutions. When the task was successfully completed, there was much cheering and self-congratulations by the team members. However, Bernie did not take part in the celebration or express any sense of satisfaction for their accomplishment.

Craig: As we reviewed the activity, I asked the group to discuss how effectively they thought they had solved the problem. Everyone, except Bernie, was extremely excited and proud of their accomplishment. Statements like, "We cooked that one," or "We really used all our resources" summed up their comments. I asked Bernie to share his observations. He stunned his fellow team members when he said, "You sounded like a bunch of magpies.

It was a solutions war, with each member trying to outdo the other and nobody listening to anyone else. Furthermore, I had no idea of what was going on, what we were doing, or why we were doing it. I was completely out of the loop, and nobody seemed to notice or care."

Following his statement there was a long silence—highly unusual for that group. Suddenly, the president spoke up. "This must be the way the rest of the people in our organization feel. They can't see what's going on, and we just tell them what to do!" That started a conversation (they actually *listened* to each other) that lasted for about forty-five minutes. They discussed the impact of their behavior and the changes they needed to make. By the end of the processing, they decided to literally turn the organizational pyramid upside down, agreeing that they would still set direction but would concentrate on empowering their employees to devise their own solutions and take action. This is a perfect example of the mileage a team can get out of one activity, reflecting and relating their actions during a contrived activity to the overall organizational reality.

At the end of the two days of team building, we asked each participant to share what the overall experience had meant to them as individuals and as a group. The newest member of the team summed it up by saying, "I've gotten to know you people better in these two days than I ever knew the people I worked with for seven years. Based on what I see in this team, I truly made the right decision to join it, and I'm incredibly proud to be here."

Later, the CEO shared with us that the business meeting that followed the team program was the most productive they had ever experienced. When asked about what changes had taken place in the organization since the program, he mentioned that the new organizational structure and the empowerment of people throughout the ranks were first met with skepticism and anxiety. Employees initially suspected that something had gone wrong in the organization and that the new structure would be used to blame them for any failures. But when people realized that the leadership group was sincere, and that there were no ulterior motives, they answered the challenge willingly. The CEO asked us to work with each of the subsidiary companies to help them understand the new approach. We embarked on a series of the most effective and enjoyable programs we ever experienced, and the company thrived for many years.

Pat: In light of the success of this incredibly important project, Craig and I could see huge potential for the experiential approach to building teams. Although I was never totally comfortable with the free-flowing unpredictability, I saw the value the programs produced. On the other hand, this programming was a perfect fit for Craig's abilities. He intuitively knows how to set up an activity to highlight a particular strength or expose a weakness of a team. And we witnessed time and again the value the team garners by discovering and discussing important issues and adjusting their roles and business procedures accordingly.

In the mideighties, most experiential ropes courses were being built at outdoor camps, usually nonprofit camps for kids. Camp directors saw the great potential of bringing in corporate dollars by offering outdoor adventure team building experiences to all kinds of organizations. These team programs were usually facilitated by camp staff, most of whom had no corporate experience. While they provided an enjoyable and interesting outing for a corporate team, the experience often didn't produce the kind of breakthrough thinking we described previously mainly because the focus was on the *activity* rather than on the *team*. The norm was for facilitators to conduct a twenty- or thirty-minute activity, allowing five minutes of group conversation at its conclusion. Craig prefers to set up a five-minute activity and spend twenty or thirty minutes discussing how the team's performance relates to the way things are done in the workplace. That process has yielded many important breakthroughs.

Pat: Eventually, I became more comfortable with the experiential programs. Even though I seldom facilitated the activities alone, I could still play an active role. We almost always use a personality inventory in conjunction with an experiential program, and I thoroughly enjoy our joint presentation of those concepts. People watching the two of us in action can easily observe our differences making it easier for them to identify their own traits and profiles. It also helps others see the advantages of working in conjunction with people who have different talents. Our clients often comment on our ability to utilize our opposing strengths. I take care of the details—making program arrangements, developing written materials, and keeping things on schedule—while Craig chooses just the right activity to make a point and leads the group in productive discussions.

Another memorable experience occurred with a multinational group of about thirty-five corporate executives who were participating in a CEO development program. For several years, we conducted a team building session as part of the curriculum for a university's executive program. It was an immersion course and the participants lived on-site for a six-week period. Our portion of the program was a half-day session conducted at the university's outdoor experiential facility, with the primary purpose of helping participants get to know each other, since they would be working together in groups for the next six weeks.

Although we had suggested that the experiential program would be more effective if it occurred early in the first week of the course, the faculty insisted on scheduling it at the beginning of the second week. The evening before our session, one of the professors hosted a cookout at his home, which we attended along with all of the participants. We noted during the evening that there was little interaction even though the group had been together for a week. They stood in line for their food, chatting occasionally among themselves or with the course professors, but there was no feeling of energy or camaraderie.

The following morning we arrived at the Graduate Center classroom where we briefly discussed the general goals of the outdoor experience in which they were about to participate. Despite their many questions, we were purposefully vague about what they would actually be doing for the rest of the morning. At the conclusion of our introduction, the participants were directed to the bus that would transport them to the outdoor recreational facility.

It was interesting to observe the group dynamics as people waited to board the bus. As CEOs, they were used to being in control, and it was obvious that most of them were ill at ease and out of their element in this situation where they had no idea what lay ahead. A few talked on their cell phones, but most were silent. They were obviously anxious at not knowing what would be expected of them. Later in the program, we described our observations and pointed out that their employees probably experience that same discomfort on a daily basis since they are often asked to carry out requests without being privy to all the information or reasoning behind it.

Pat: Given the diverse group of people and the short period of time we had to work with them, it was a challenge for us to determine what activities would be most effective and meaningful. We started with a couple of icebreakers and warm-up activities to relax the group and get them beyond their initial anxiety. Then we introduced an activity called the Mute Lineup. The directions were simple—all the participants were to line up according to their date of birth (month and day) starting with January

1 and ending with December 31. As the name of the activity implies, no one was able to speak throughout the entire exercise.

For a while, there was little action as participants pondered their assignment. Finally, a few brave souls began trying to interact by using gestures. Eventually, they realized that they could communicate by holding up fingers to indicate the month and day of their birth. The atmosphere was chaotic with so many people who were used to assuming the leadership position, but eventually, a few folks took the lead and directed others as to what position they should take in the line. Their confidence grew as more people took their places, and finally, although some individuals still seemed confused and unsure, the majority of the group indicated they were satisfied that they had lined up in the proper order.

Craig: We asked them to stay in their positions while each person, from the beginning to the end of the line, shared their birth date with the rest of the group. By the third or fourth person, it became obvious that their lineup was not in consecutive order. Then it began to dawn on the participants what had happened. While in some countries, such as the United States, we list the month first and then the day, other countries do the opposite. The group had experienced a simple but profound example of how difficult it can be to communicate with individuals from different backgrounds despite the fact that they thought they had agreed upon a "common language."

The participants discussed at length the effects such differences can have on international business relations. We provided them with several additional challenges, each one requiring more interaction and cooperation than the last. By the time the group boarded the bus for their return to the university, they looked like they had been to summer camp. There was a great deal of interaction, laughter, and camaraderie, which carried forward through the remainder of their time together.

We were fortunate to be invited to design and deliver programs for several of the organizations represented at the CEO development program. Months later, as we were interacting with one of those participants, he told us that because of the outdoor experience, he and one of the other CEOs had spent a great deal of time talking with each other and had eventually formed a business partnership as well as a lasting friendship. This story clearly indicates that the key advantage of experiential programming is not the experience itself, but the conversations and insights such activities generate.

Our reputation in the field of team building and experiential programming began to grow, and we were contacted by a large information technology organization to design and facilitate a program for approximately 180 of their employees, all of whom worked on the same project from locations throughout the United States and Europe. The vice president in charge of that project thought they could achieve greater efficiencies if members of the team got to know each other as more than just voices on the telephone. Since the collective group was much too large for any type of meaningful experience, we suggested dividing them into three smaller groups and repeating the same format and activities three times.

We decided to utilize a personality inventory to determine each person's preferred operating style. The emphasis throughout the program was focused on communication, and the inventory gave the entire project team a common language for understanding and discussing their similarities and differences. In addition, we planned a number of indoor and outdoor experiential activities to help individuals get to know each other and enhance their effectiveness.

Pat: The entire program took place over one week—three waves of sixty people for two days each. Craig and I and two other facilitators worked with the groups through six straight days of programming. It was a young, bright, and energetic group of individuals, and they participated wholeheartedly in every aspect of the program. They delighted in getting to know the people they had previously interacted with only by phone or e-mail. And, although each group only got to know 60 of their 180 counterparts, their participation in the same activities gave them a common experience to discuss during future phone and personal interactions.

One very simple yet valuable activity required each of the small groups of fifteen to decide on a group name, design a group cheer, and sing a signature song, which they performed for the larger group. It was an excellent means for the participants to connect names with faces. The groups were quite creative and enjoyed performing as well as encouraging other performances. Years later, people within that organization still remember their group names and songs.

The participants were predominantly male, and we initially observed during problem-solving activities, that input from the outnumbered females were either not heard or not considered. We even noticed that, when confronted with a challenge, the men gathered around the area in a tight circle to discuss the problem, making it impossible for the women to see the challenge or contribute to the solution.

Craig: We decided to highlight the fact that they were missing valuable input, so we modified our Islands activity and named it the Bud Lite Islands. The islands—a series of three platforms in the midst of "shark-infested waters"—had to be traversed by each group. It required considerable planning to accomplish successfully, and we introduced an added challenge: As each group arrived on the islands, all males lost their ability to speak, plan, or use their arms. The women were in charge of planning and assuring that everyone safely reached their destination. They did a great job, and when the challenge was complete, their discussions were very valuable. The men had been unaware that they were excluding the women and realized that they probably had the same tendency at work. It was a valuable lesson for everyone, especially the males, as they observed the effective problem solving skills of their female counterparts.

Each evening, we conducted enjoyable, lighthearted activities such as a Dutch Auction and talent shows. The participation was enthusiastic, creative, and enjoyable. As facilitators, we were exhausted at the end of the six days, but it was a satisfying feeling. While this project required days of planning and plenty of hard mental and physical work—especially developing and overseeing the complex logistics—it was one of the most successful and memorable programs of our years in business. The IT organization was delighted with the results and reported enhanced effectiveness in their ability to accomplish their work and serve their customers.

Pat: Another organization that truly astounded us with their energy and enthusiasm was a county court system, including all the administrators and judges. We expected the group would be serious and somewhat stuffy to work with and were pleasantly surprised the judges had any interest in participating in such a program. Our preconceptions were totally wrong.

Once again, we utilized an operating style inventory to help participants understand their own strengths and the collective strengths of the group.

During the program, group members chose to share their profiles and were quite surprised by the differences, especially among the judges. The administrators found the information especially enlightening and helpful for their interaction with each other and with each individual judge. The judges were able to see the implications of their individual styles on how they approached their judicial responsibilities. Using these insights, all of the participants developed more effective and efficient ways to organize and carry out their respective duties.

This two-day program included an overnight stay at a state park facility. The court administrator had arranged for karaoke as the evening's entertainment, and we weren't quite sure what to expect. It turned out to be a lively and entertaining evening with everyone actively participating despite varying degrees of musical ability. The administrative judge did a solo rendition of "Danny Boy" in celebration of his Irish heritage. We three facilitators joined in as well, performing "Little Red Riding Hood." Those memories still bring smiles.

Soon afterward, we were contacted by the administrator of a sizeable East Coast law firm. We were told that the firm was suffering from a lack of cohesiveness partially brought on by its physical setup. The firm consisted of multiple practice areas scattered throughout several floors of a large office building. In our conversations with the firm administrator, we learned that the attorneys mainly interacted with others in their own practice group, and there was little cross-communication. Both the administrator and the managing partners were concerned they were missing out on valuable opportunities because the practice groups were so isolated—both physically and psychologically. After some discussion, we agreed to develop and conduct a three-day retreat at an off-site location with emphasis on communication and cooperation.

We weren't surprised to learn that most of the attorneys were skeptical of any process that might be considered touchy-feely. They were also reluctant to spend time in any pursuits that didn't produce billable hours. The firm had not participated in a retreat for several years, and we got some vibes that the past retreat had not gone well. Only after our program did we learn how disastrous the previous retreat had been. It was no wonder that many participants approached this process with such skepticism.

Since skeptics are more likely to accept data they produce themselves, we asked the participants to complete the MBTI and our Team Assessment Survey in preparation for the retreat. The MBTI provided a snapshot of the operating styles of the team members while the TAS highlighted the strengths and vulnerabilities of the overall practice. That information was invaluable as we designed the content and flow of the program.

Pat: The retreat was held off-site in a resort hotel. The atmosphere was decidedly chilly as we entered the conference room that first morning. Some folks talked quietly in groups of two or three while others were busy with cell phones and PDAs. Several stood alone exhibiting the arms-crossed stance that dared anyone to tell them anything they didn't already know. Though not an entirely unusual scenario at the start of a program, this group was more openly cynical than most. We knew we had our work cut out for us.

Craig: We began the day with some initial icebreakers and warm-up activities, but nothing too frivolous in nature for this group. Then we introduced the Myers-Briggs information. Their MBTI group profile explained many of the things that were mentioned on the TAS as being barriers to working together. We hoped that an understanding of their profile would break down some of those barriers.

We interspersed the MBTI processing with experiential activities to allow the group to demonstrate for themselves the principles of type. Gradually, the level of interest heightened as participants began to see many parallels between the data and their interactions at work. Even more interest was generated when they agreed to share their individual results by filling in a "best fit" type table. We invited each of the participants to register their "best fit" type on an overhead slide, assigning different colored markers to the various practice areas. There was increasing conversation and even laughter as the participants observed emerging patterns. It became evident that attorneys in the same practice areas shared very similar MBTI preferences. And the different practice areas were clustered in different quadrants of the type table. No wonder there was a communication issue! Knowing that attorneys like to figure things out for themselves, we asked them, based on the MBTI results, what they thought would be the strengths and weaknesses of any team with such a profile. They recorded that information on flip chart paper as the final activity of the first day.

On the second day, we reviewed the results of the TAS. The survey results and narrative comments were predictable. The lowest scores were registered for statements about working toward clear goals, awareness of how individual responsibilities relate to the overall organization, open communication, and sharing of information. They saw their strengths as confidence, aggressiveness, and energy and their key weakness as the lack of intrafirm communications. The survey results almost exactly echoed the strengths and weaknesses they had listed on the flip chart the day before.

Pat: When the lawyers considered the data generated by the MBTI and the TAS together, even the most skeptical individuals saw obvious connections. It was as if a switch flipped on, and the energy and conversation began to flow freely. In the course of discussions that followed, they even discovered that they had been referring clients to other law firms because they were unaware of all of the specialty areas represented by lawyers in their own firm!

The remainder of the retreat was spent discussing and planning ways to bring value to each other's clients, how they could more effectively market their services, and how their diversity provided strength rather than barriers. During breaks, we observed small groups huddled in the hallway, scheduling appointments to introduce clients to attorneys in other practice areas. They began discussing a formal process for considering client needs and cross-marketing opportunities. Craig and I agreed that such a transformation could never have been accomplished if the attorneys had not generated their own data.

Later that evening at the closing dinner event, the mood was lively, positive, and energetic. Only then did we learn from one of the partners about their previous retreat several years before. He told us that the earlier retreat had incorporated the California approach, which was popular at the time. That approach included getting a group to bond by divulging very personal information and utilizing what the partner described as lots of touchy-feely activities. No wonder it was five years before they agreed to take part in another retreat! We were glad we hadn't known the details of that earlier experience before we started working with the group.

Months later, we worked with a company that provided hardware and software systems and consulting services to the automotive industry. They also were experiencing the effects of poor communication between departments. The group included the sales and service operations and the interaction between the two departments bordered on hostile. The underlying issue was the compensation system. The members of the sales team were compensated according to the amount of hardware and software they sold while the service team members earned straight salaries. This situation epitomized one of our favorite sayings—"You get what you reward"!

Naturally, the sales folks weren't necessarily focused on solutions as much as they were on quantity of sales. They also weren't as well informed about the intricacies of the equipment and software. The service department was charged with making sure the hardware and software operated efficiently, which wasn't always the case. The service people were very frustrated because they bore the brunt of customer frustration while the sales team walked off with accolades and financial rewards based on the volume of products they sold—whether or not the system worked.

Craig: We designed and facilitated a day-long program with the managers of both the sales and service teams. To begin with, there was finger-pointing and sarcasm displayed by both groups. Once again, we used the MBTI and compared the profiles of the two departments. The result was a revelation to the participants. The people drawn to sales tended to be outgoing, matter-of-fact, subjective, and bottom-line oriented. The service team profile leaned toward introspection, complexity, objectivity, and reflection. No wonder they didn't communicate well!

After processing that information, we spent an afternoon engaged in problem solving activities with mixed groups of sales and service representatives. They realized that together they could accomplish a better solution for their customers than either of the groups could achieve separately. After that day and a couple of additional consulting sessions, the company decided to assign mixed teams of both sales and service representatives to all of their customer accounts. All team members were to be compensated the same—a combination of salary and sales incentives. This configuration made the best use of everyone's talents and provided a fair system of compensation. It was a win for everyone including the customers, the sales and service employees and the company.

Another opportunity for mistrust between groups occurred when one of our large clients purchased a small manufacturing company in Wisconsin. The difference in size was not the only issue. The pace, pressures, and workloads varied greatly between the two organizations, and the big city versus rural mind-set presented a major culture shock for both. They did share a common love of the outdoors—being from Colorado and Wisconsin—so a significant portion of the program we designed took place at an outdoor facility involving experiential activities.

Craig: Our Site Central exercise proved to be the most enlightening activity for the two groups. Its purpose was to help each group experience some measure of what the other group was feeling, so basically the two organizations switched roles. For purposes of the activity, the managers from Colorado (the acquiring company) were assigned the role of a "factory site" and had access to all the "materials." The Wisconsin company played the role of the "central office," which meant they were management and had access to all the "information" but no hand in the construction process. The two groups were located forty or fifty yards from each other and neither could see what the other was doing. All interaction took place through messages carried back and forth.

The factory had to build an object to the satisfaction of the central office (management). Directives were carried to the factory by one representative of management and that representative could also bring back questions from the factory about how to proceed. Other than that, there was no interaction between the two groups. It took quite a long time for them to reach the objective. Much like actual day-to-day operations, each group was in the dark as to the thinking of the other team. The Wisconsin team, accustomed to taking orders from Colorado, now understood how difficult it could be to give direction from a distance. The Colorado team now understood that they weren't always attuned to the challenges at the manufacturing site. The two teams gained insight by walking in each other's shoes, and each company experienced firsthand the frustrations of the other. From that time forward, everyone was more aware of the challenges, more informative with their directions, and more patient with one another.

In the course of that trip, we also learned something about folks in rural Wisconsin—they aren't especially accepting of people from the big city. This was most obvious when we entered a store or restaurant. Proprietors pretty much ignored people they didn't know. We waited an inordinate amount of time to be seated at a restaurant despite the absence of a crowd. When we finally were seated, it was in a cramped corner adjoining the buffet table, certainly not a private or choice location. We were brazen enough to ask to be moved, which didn't endear us to the hostess. Dinner was very tasty, but the service was not warm, and once again, we were ignored when we went to the pay the cashier.

Pat: While Craig was waiting to pay the check, I glanced at the Green Bay Packers football game on the TV behind the bar. Being a passionate football enthusiast, I commented positively about an impressive play that Brett Favre had just orchestrated. That's all it took! Everyone around the bar began talking to me as if I were a lifelong friend. For the rest of the time we were in town we made a point of mentioning how well the Packers had played on Sunday, and our level of service improved significantly.

We thought we were experiencing the same phenomenon several months later when we did a program for a pet food manufacturing plant in rural North Carolina. Once again, there was really only one nice restaurant in town, so we went there twice for dinner. We noticed both times that we were *not* seated in the main dining area (although there were plenty of tables available) but in a small room off to the side. We thought it was a little strange but didn't understand why until we got home and started to unpack our suitcases. All of our clothes smelled like the brewer's yeast the company uses during the manufacturing process. Having spent each day in the plant, we became conditioned to the odor of our own clothing. But apparently, it had been quite noticeable to those around us!

Craig: Many times it's the attitude of the group or the way you choose to view a particular situation that turns an ordinary experience into a meaningful one. I facilitated a program for the customer service department of a company that produces baby products. Most of the calls they received were from dissatisfied and often irate customers. They found themselves frequently discouraged and out of sorts as they wondered how to cope with such constant negativity. After a bit of brainstorming, they decided that each week they would have a contest to determine who had the rudest, most outrageous customer. Every person in the department contributed $5 to the "kitty" each Monday. On Friday afternoon, they all sat down together while each person shared their worst horror story of the week. The person with the most outrageous story won the kitty. From that time forward, they didn't mind the verbal abuse quite so much since it meant they might win the jackpot. That's one way of turning lemons into lemonade.

Here are some tips for designing and facilitating a worthwhile experience, whether working with organizations or training other facilitators.

How to experience more magic

- Conduct a careful investigation of the group and its needs by gathering information from people at all levels who will be participating in a program.
- Carefully plan programs and customize them for each group's unique style and needs.
- Plan experiences and activities that echo real-life and work situations.
- Be flexible during programs—react and adjust to the needs of the group.
- Spend time in meaningful discussions rather than rushing from one activity to another. Discussion is the catalyst for breakthrough thinking.
- Don't allow the behavior of one or two people to dominate the group's perspective.
- The key focus is always on the group, never on the facilitator.
- Celebrate the successes with the team and savor the magic moments!

CHAPTER 6

Make Your Own Rules

Our approach to running our business may be unconventional, but it works well for us. While we often ignore common business practices and "business school" advice, we hasten to add that we always abide by all legal and accounting regulations. We also have excellent advisors who make sure everything is in proper order. But outside of those parameters, we most often follow a path that appeals to our talents and instincts and, most of all, to our hearts.

Do we do everything perfectly? Certainly not! Have we been as financially successful as we might have been? No! But we have run the business in a way that makes the best use of our styles and values. By that measure, we couldn't have done much better. Despite the colossal differences in our approaches, most of the time we agree on the course of action to take. When we don't agree, each of us is amenable to deferring to the one who has the most experience, the best track record with the particular subject at hand, or the strongest gut feeling about how we ought to proceed.

A large part of the reason we started our own business was to have the freedom to do things the way we believed they should be done. Craig has very little patience with rules that don't make sense. That became evident soon after he accepted his university administrative position. When he came to the university to manage the career planning and placement department, the facilities had just been relocated and had undergone a significant remodeling process. One morning Craig received a phone call from one of the university deans, who said there was a serious issue that had come to his attention, and he needed to discuss it. Craig said he would be happy to discuss any issue and invited Dean Jones to come to his office.

Craig: Dean Jones was very nervous when he arrived. He spent several minutes talking about generalities, and I finally asked him to share what was on his mind. He stated nervously, "Well, Craig, you see, you have a window in your office." I nodded and answered that I was well aware of my window. He then explained that his assistant dean did not have a window in his office. I nodded again and continued to listen, wondering where this discussion was going. After some more prompting, Dean Jones finally voiced his concern. I was considered to be below the level of an assistant dean largely because they were usually faculty members who had earned their doctorate degrees. Even though I was a department head, I only had a master's degree and was not a faculty member, so I was not entitled to have a window. Having never been in a university setting before, this hierarchical attitude was foreign to me.

I successfully controlled my anger and dismay and simply asked him what he thought I should do about the situation since this was the office space to which I had been assigned, and it just happened to have a window. He had no answer for that question and continued to repeat his premise that I definitely was not at the level to have a window. Trying to introduce some humor into an otherwise ridiculous situation, I asked if he would feel better if I covered my window with cardboard. His reaction confirmed my suspicion that he was humorless and somewhat befuddled by my question. I finally got up from my chair and announced that I needed to get back to work. I told him as diplomatically as possible to let me know if he thought of a way for me to comply with the "unwritten rule" regarding windows. I never heard from him again regarding that subject.

That obsession with rules occurs in many organizations but seemed especially rampant in the university system at that time. Several years later, Craig moved from the career planning department to the continuing education department within the same university As is his nature, he approached the new assignment full of excitement with lots of ideas for innovative programming and new ways to enhance the current course offerings. After a few weeks on the job, he met with the dean to share some of these ideas and was told, in no uncertain terms, that he would be willing to listen to Craig's ideas—only after Craig had about ten years of experience at continuing ed under his belt! Craig described his feelings about the incident, saying, "The switch suddenly went off."

Pat: I could tell when Craig walked in the door that evening that all of his inspiration and excitement over his new job was gone, and I knew he would soon be miserable without an outlet for his creativity. Those kinds of situations strengthened our desire to pursue a business of our own. A few months later, after reviewing and discussing our finances, we agreed it was time for Craig to leave the university system and take over Career Resources full-time. While a bit frightening to a person as risk averse as I am, I knew it was the right decision.

Our approach to running our own company might not qualify us as poster children for a business school, but it could be very appropriate material for an ethics course. We not only concentrate on what makes the best use of our own talents and appeals to our values, we also focus on doing what is right for our clients, whether we are dealing with individuals or corporations. Confidentiality has always been one of our primary guiding principles. We have been able to serve outplacement clients *and* their former companies with equal diligence while keeping all information totally confidential on both sides. Later, as we moved into working with teams and coaching executives, we have continued that loyalty and confidentiality with every person involved in each process.

While we started our business in an unconventional fashion, we weren't without business experience. Craig had managed a boating retail business, and Pat had been an office manager and bookkeeper for a small high-tech firm before she accepted the job as financial and administrative manager at a large public accounting firm. That position provided her with great insight into the workings of much larger companies. In addition, both of us had worked in our fathers' businesses, learning many valuable lessons along the way. Pat's father was an attorney in a single practice. Craig's father owned a sizeable public relations firm with offices in several large cities. We learned different lessons from working with our fathers and were able to incorporate that collective knowledge into the way we approach our own business.

Pat: My father was a small town lawyer, and his practice was primarily in the areas of tax, real estate, and estate law. When he started out, he had no office and met clients in the local coffee shop to transact business. When I was as young as five, I would accompany him when he went to the homes of rural clients in the evenings to discuss wills or have documents signed. From age twelve through high school, I did typing and bookkeeping for him. Besides finding out I was good at bookkeeping and a lousy typist, I learned the importance of confidentiality, accuracy, honesty, integrity, and reputation—all of which were important to our success when Craig and I started our business.

Craig: I was too young to remember when my father left his public relations job with a major corporation to start his own business. The family legend is that when he discussed his plans with my mother, explaining that they had less than $2,000 in the bank to work with, she said "You just wait and see how far I can make $2,000 go!" I worked briefly with my father whose firm by that time represented some of the country's largest manufacturers of kitchen and household appliances. I mainly wrote promotional copy for trade shows and industry meetings. Being as people oriented as I am, I had difficulty getting excited about a frost-free freezer or a new promotional campaign, but I did absorb some good sound business practices, including the importance of a business's reputation and the care one must take with each client.

Primarily, we each saw that our fathers, as business owners, had the opportunity to do things the way they wanted them done. While they answered to their clients, they were at liberty to run their businesses as they saw fit in ways that made the best use of their strengths and talents. We both wanted that opportunity. Even though at first we weren't clear about what the focus of our business would be, we were sure it would involve helping people make the most of their talents. We also knew that it would give *us* the opportunity to operate in the way that made the best use of *our* collective talents.

We don't necessarily recommend that others follow our approach to establishing or running a business, but it worked well for us and yielded many interesting lessons. What we *do* recommend is that people take time to determine what it is that they love to do and are good at doing and try to incorporate as many of those attributes as possible into their job description, whether working for themselves or for others. We started Career Resources with $300, a dream, and the confidence we had gained from our fathers. We had optimism, knowledge, excitement, inspiration, and the desire to help people discover what they loved to do. And along the way, we disregarded just about every word of advice about building a business that was ever written.

First of all, we have never had a business plan. It's difficult to write a business plan when you're not sure what your business is, and for a couple of years, we had lots of ideas and talents, but no clear focus. One positive thing about not having a plan was that it allowed us to experiment with several different concepts. What we *did* have from the very beginning—due to Craig's vast knowledge and cutting-edge approach to career development—was the ability to help people determine their strengths, skills, desires, and capabilities. It just wasn't clear how we could earn a living with that expertise.

We thoroughly explored our own strengths and capabilities, and armed with that self-knowledge, we were able to seize the opportunity that presented itself when major corporate downsizing turned outplacement consulting into a lucrative business. Perhaps if we'd been following a business plan, we might have missed out on that opportunity. Even after we found our niche and business was booming, we continued to shun the idea of a business plan. To this day, we operate without such a document.

We've never had a strategic plan either. The absence of such a plan actually made it easier for us to adjust our focus several times as we became aware of needs that weren't being met and opportunities to approach situations in unconventional ways. Craig operates best when he's inspired. The thought of doing the same thing in the same way for years can squelch his creativity. It was natural for him to continually push the envelope and venture into new areas, which became a major advantage for us in an ever-changing business environment. So, in hindsight, we can claim that our business strategy has been to take advantage of new opportunities when they present themselves, so long as they mesh with our strengths, needs, and desires.

Sometimes our unconventional approach led to working ourselves *out* of business. In the case of team development, our goal is to provide tools and processes for a team so they can work together effectively and accomplish more. Once team members have grasped that concept and have learned the processes necessary to reach that goal, the team can do things on their own without our guidance. The same is true with executive coaching. We provide clients with all the tools needed to enhance their effectiveness, and then they no longer need our help. Fortunately, our clients are our best marketers, and we end up working with other teams and individuals within the same organization or with other organizations that have heard about us from our clients. Word of mouth suffices as our marketing plan—yet another document we have never developed.

Pat: Marketing was one area where we did seek some guidance. At one time, I had been part of the management team of a small organization that had used a marketing consultant. Craig and I decided that developing such a plan would be beneficial in helping to jump-start our new business. We sought advice from the same consultant with rather horrifying results. After several sessions that weren't especially productive, the consultant made a very inappropriate advance to me with Craig sitting right in the same room. We were out of his office in a flash and never returned! That's as far as we ever got with formal marketing, but we became very creative in developing ways to spread the word about our business.

One marketing idea we tried early on with great success was hosting lunchtime discussions among human resource professionals from local organizations. These were individuals we had met through a human resources professional association. We invited three or four people per gathering to our office and suggested a specific topic of common interest to explore during our time together. Lunch often consisted of hot roast beef sandwiches or homemade soup we prepared in our Crock-Pot—definitely a low-budget affair. The response from attendees was very enthusiastic, and the discussions were fun and enlightening for everyone. We established collegial relationships with key professionals in many large organizations while learning what human resource issues were most important. It was a way of bringing people together and gaining their trust and respect without any hard selling, and it led to lots of business opportunities.

Later, as we moved into the team development phase of our business, we created a board of advisors made up of top managers and executives from organizations that had experienced our programs. We made a conscious decision to use advisors rather than establish a board of directors. Advisors offer ideas that can be used or discarded. Directors give mandates that must be followed, and we chose not to hand over that control. Our advisors kept us abreast of the latest thinking on many subjects within mid- to large-sized corporations, and we often adjusted our programming and marketing approaches based on their input. We also knew enough at this point to determine when to follow advice and when to follow our own heads and hearts.

Craig: By this time, we knew we needed a professional-looking brochure or "leave-behind" piece to explain our programs, especially as we added team development to the services we offered. Team development was a very new concept at the time, and it was important to explain it effectively. We hired a marketing professional to develop and produce a brochure for us. Her first approach was to interview us about the programs we designed and facilitated. The copy she produced as a result of that attempt was nice, but it lacked something that we really wanted to convey. We all agreed that, while it accurately described what we did, it just didn't capture the way we did it—with warmth and enthusiasm. We suggested to our marketing person that she interview some folks who had actually experienced each of the services we offered. Much to our delight, their comments clearly conveyed the warm personal relationships that we build with our clients. The resulting brochure was exactly what we wanted, and it served us well for at least ten years. Even though we no longer use it as a marketing piece, since we no longer offer some of the services that it describes, we often share a copy with new clients to give them a feeling for the way we approach our work in general.

We also produced a quarterly newsletter that served as a terrific marketing tool. It included book reviews, a question-and-answer section, and articles on hot topics in the human resources field. It was an excellent piece to include with our brochure, client list, and introductory letter when we were meeting with prospective or first-time clients.

Pat: I love to write, and the newsletter provided a creative outlet for me while providing clients and prospects with leading edge information about human resource and training issues. Some of the main articles have explored topics such as networking skills, use of assessment tools, interviewing tips, productivity, and teamwork. It also provides a way to share some of the data we gather from our TAS about how employees view the workplace.

Over the years, we have received some wonderful publicity, both individually and for our company with little or no effort on our part. Craig was featured in several articles when he instituted career planning workshops at Wright State University. He was also interviewed on television several times offering tips and advice to job seekers. Our company began gaining press coverage starting in 1980 when the daily newspaper covered our first seminars on career change, and later, there were several stories about the outplacement boom, which included quotes from Craig. Together we were featured in a full-page spread as one of three couples interviewed for an article about married couples who had developed their own businesses. We received some publicity when we opened our second outplacement office and again when we facilitated one of our first outdoor experiential programs for a large Dayton-based corporation. We were featured in several chamber of commerce newsletters and were interviewed on television regarding the Leadership Dayton program. This free publicity provided invaluable marketing opportunities.

Our involvement as retreat facilitators and program directors for community leadership programs throughout Ohio—and in several other states—provides some of our best marketing opportunities. For years, we facilitated the opening and closing retreats for local and statewide leadership programs. Craig currently conducts the retreats for as many as eight leadership programs annually throughout the country. These opportunities give us annual exposure to at least two hundred high-level managers and corporate executives as well as many not-for-profit organizations and have resulted in numerous business opportunities.

We gained several pieces of business as a result of being part of the university CEO development and human resource executive development programs. The fact that we are both qualified in the use of the Myers-Briggs Type Indicator and several other assessment instruments has also attracted clients. We are well known within the MBTI community, and when companies or individuals request a program in our geographic location, the organization that publishes the MBTI instrument may refer them to us. All of these networks have resulted in numerous business opportunities while requiring a limited investment of time and money.

Pat: Other marketing tools that work well for us include: our extensive volunteer work, speeches and presentations for professional groups and nonprofit events, word of mouth, former program participants who move to new organizations and recommend our programs, and Craig's amazing gift of engaging in conversations with total strangers! He comes home from every trip—be it business or pleasure—with several business cards and the life stories of all those who were fortunate enough to sit beside him on his flights. He never tries to sell to anyone and mostly listens to their stories, but folks are always interested in the programs and processes we provide and the huge variety of organizations we have served. The excitement for our work that he conveys is infectious. We also notice that people are drawn to the fact that we are a husband-and-wife team whose business has thrived for many years. The most common comment we hear on that subject is, "My spouse and I could NEVER work together!"

Most of our marketing effort is really just exhibiting our genuine interest in people. If, while talking with someone, we learn about a need they have, we're happy to give them suggestions. Sometimes that includes describing our services; other times it results in a referral to some other organization, service, or resource material. Craig's theory about our business is that we are an "aspirin," and we should look for people with a "headache." If they have a "stomachache," we refer them to someone who treats that condition. In the long run, people really appreciate that approach and remember our enthusiasm. And if they know someone with a headache, they are very likely to refer them to us.

When it comes to money management, we're also unconventional. We have never had a financial plan. Craig doesn't want to know how much money we have in the bank because he never wants to feel that he has to sell a piece of business because of *our* need versus the needs of the client. It doesn't really work to try to project what our income might be in any given year. Some years we have a few very large clients, and other years we have lots of smaller programs. Since 1996 our offices have been in our home, so there is very little overhead. And now that we are the only employees of our corporation, we can adjust our salaries to fit the circumstances. Pat keeps a very close eye on the money situation, and Craig knows an alarm will be sounded if we are ever anywhere close to financial difficulty.

When we started the business, we pledged that we would never borrow money. We broke our promise once but only in order to establish a favorable credit rating. We borrowed a small amount using our own cash as collateral and paid it back over the course of a year. We used the borrowed money to buy some stock, which gave us a greater rate of return than the interest we paid on the loan. Without the need to borrow money, no one ever asks to see a financial plan.

Pat: We also have never had a budget. I have to admit that bothers me a bit; after all, I was the financial manager for a public accounting firm! For several years, I suggested to Craig that we develop a budget, and he always agreed that that was a good idea. But he could never give me meaningful figures for any of the budget categories. And since we're both very conservative spenders, it just didn't seem to be a real necessity. After a few years, I stopped worrying about it.

Craig: I never want to know how much money we have. I'd rather accept or reject a piece of business based on whether it's right for the client and a match for our expertise, rather than accepting it because we need the money. If I suggest a purchase and Pat says, "We probably shouldn't right now," that's fine. If I really insist, Pat knows it's an important item, and she'll find a way to make the purchase. We make all our major spending decisions together, including charitable donations, which are very important to both of us. We are committed to giving back to the community that has supported us for more than twenty-five years. At the end of each year, we calculate the amount of funds we can comfortably donate, Pat and I each make a list of charities we want to support, and we determine our gifts accordingly.

The most problematic financial issue for us has always been pricing our services. When we were in the outplacement business, pricing was not as difficult. Fees were calculated as a percentage of the salary of the individual executive with whom we were working. The percentage amount was fairly standard throughout the industry until the bidding wars began. But when we changed our focus to team building and leadership development, pricing decisions weren't so easy.

Pat: As usual, we approach the pricing issue from two different perspectives. I'm inclined to calculate a fee based on what it costs to develop and deliver a piece of business. Craig's approach is to price according to what the product is worth to the client. We both tend to underprice the value of our services. At first, we considered pricing our team building programs in line with what the outdoor adventure facilities were charging. It was a significant breakthrough when we realized that, while the camp facilitators were schooled in the mechanics of directing outdoor activities, they didn't have the business experience to relate those activities to business realities. At that point, we changed the pricing of our team programs dramatically to reflect the professional experience and insights that we bring to each team process and the amount of time we spend with the client assessing their needs and desired outcomes. Even with that adjustment, we probably still underpriced our services, judging from the fact that we've lost only a handful of potential projects due to pricing!

Collecting money from clients was never an issue until recently. In twenty-five years of business, we never required signed contracts and never had a problem with receiving payment. Because we work so closely and collaboratively with a client, we form a close bond, and withholding payment would be like stealing from a friend. There has only been one instance when we weren't paid for our work. That involved an individual client who had consulted with us for career planning services. She didn't complete the process and paid only for a portion of the services we had delivered. The outstanding amount was about $200—not a major loss, but still disconcerting.

In 2005, after a couple of instances of very tardy payments, we decided to require signed contracts, stating the scope of services, delivery dates, and terms of payment. This was in reaction to the practices of one of our largest clients who, without warning, instituted the policy of delaying payments for at least three months after billing, sometimes longer. At that time, our work with them represented about 70 percent of our billings—a considerable sum of money that could have been earning interest for us. Our objections were met with a polite "it's our company policy." Occasional prodding helped a bit, but our only recourse was to live with the reality while seeking other clients. We pay our own bills in thirty days or less. The small amount of interest we might earn by delaying payment doesn't make up for the lack of fairness.

One planning item that might have been helpful is a human resources plan. We were consistently unsuccessful in predicting our needs in that area partially because we changed our business focus several times as the environment, and our own interests and needs changed. The number of people we needed and the expertise we required were significantly different at different points in time. An additional factor was that we both prefer working directly with clients rather than managing other people who work with our clients. Those considerations limited our success in hiring and retaining employees other than administrative staff.

Craig: There were other reasons that influenced our inability to find the right employees. First of all, we've been on the leading edge of the field each time our business focus has changed. As a result, there were few experienced people available when we needed them in career development, team building, or executive coaching. With a company our size, it's difficult to take time to train someone when we are both stretched to the limit. Secondly, our clients wanted to work directly with us and were often unhappy if we assigned someone else to a project. Thirdly, we admit that we aren't very good at finding and retaining the right people because we tend to see the potential in others rather than the actual skills and motivations they currently possess. Our blind spot has been our assumption that other people are as motivated as we are. Lastly, we are both perfectionists and control freaks when it comes to our business. After all, it's our name that is on the door!

Despite a few glitches here and there, our unconventional approach to running our business has served us well. But our circumstances are unusual. Just like the pharmaceutical ads, we urge you "not to try this without consulting your business advisors"! We started our business by taking stock of our own talents, dreams, and desires. We apply that approach to our clients by learning everything we can about them and their situation before we make any recommendations. We customize every piece of work we do for both teams and individuals. It's a process that is time intensive and limits our profitability. But, in our estimation, this approach produces a superior product, which is the only way we care to operate. That's the choice that fits our styles. To be effective, each consultant and business person must determine their own style and their own parameters and make their choices accordingly.

Suggestions about making your own rules

- Seek a job or create your own business atmosphere that allows you to do what you really enjoy doing and to work in the ways you prefer to work.
- Find great advisors—banker, attorney, and accountant at the very least—who really care about you and your success.
- Seek input but follow your heart. You're the only person who knows what is best and most appropriate for you.
- Get involved in the community—not just for visibility but to give back to the community that supports you and your business.
- Always give people more than they expect.

Chapter 7

Expect the Unexpected

No matter how diligent you are in gathering information from clients or how thoroughly you map out a program, when you're dealing with people the unexpected is bound to happen. We've had plenty of surprises! Some involved glitches with equipment or problems at a facility. Those were usually minor, even humorous annoyances, that were easily resolved. Others were curveballs from participants that caught us unaware and required adjustments to the plan. But the worst surprises of all are the "setups" that result from someone's personal agenda.

We've conducted programs in hundreds of different facilities throughout the United States and Canada with varying levels of satisfaction and a shock or two. At one point, a local camp we often used for experiential and ropes course programs decided to hire a marketing person unbeknownst to us. While this action shouldn't have had any impact on customers who were using the facility, this woman appeared to lack the appropriate social skills. She also apparently neglected to read the chapter on ethics in her marketing manual. Dressed in a navy blue suit and high heels and clutching her brochures, she attempted to market to our clients *while* they were participating in outdoor group activities. Although disconcerting, inappropriate, and highly unethical, it was a rather humorous sight to see her tripping around in high heels while people were walking on balance beams and climbing ropes. We brought the intrusion to the attention of the facility's director, and the next time we were at the site, the marketing person was nowhere to be seen.

You would expect that people who book facilities at hotels and retreat centers would ask questions about the noise level of each program and assign rooms accordingly, but our experience indicates that they don't. Several times, we've been assigned to rooms, divided only by a sliding partition, that are right next to very noisy groups. Once, we were adjacent to a gospel singing group—beautiful music but impossible to conduct a program nearby. Another time we were next to a McDonalds "motivational gathering"—use your imagination on that one. In both cases, there were no other meeting rooms available for us to make a move. Fortunately, we were able to take our groups outside to conduct activities and have meaningful discussions in peace. These experiences prompted us to monitor the noise level of our own programs. People have a lot of fun in our sessions, and we try to find space that won't impact others or at least make sure we keep the volume down so as not to be disruptive.

Each August, we facilitate a retreat for about forty people participating in a local community leadership program. A lovely state park facility is the site for the two-day program. One of the group challenges is an orienteering activity, which requires teams to use maps and compasses to locate items placed throughout the park area. A few years ago, we arrived at the site to discover that we were sharing the park facility with a bow hunters convention whose participants were actively hunting deer on the park grounds! We quickly huddled with the park officials to make sure the hunters were confined to one area of the park, while our group was assigned to another area a safe distance away. The leadership group listened VERY intently as we emphasized that they were not to cross the road that divided the two areas. We also provided bright yellow bandanas, which were accepted and worn with enthusiasm. Everyone returned safely, and the participants took great delight in recounting their "dangerous adventure" to friends and family.

Craig: People often return from camps and outdoor programs with interesting stories of the trials and tribulations of roughing it. I facilitated a two-day program for the management team of a small engineering firm. There was only one woman on the team, and she was assigned her own cabin while all the men shared a second cabin nearby. In the middle of the night, the men were awakened by the young woman yelling for someone to come help her. Not knowing the nature of her need, the males hurriedly obliged—en masse. They found their female teammate standing on her bed pointing at a mouse. The men shooed the mouse outside, and all was well for the remainder of the night. The story became a company legend!

Considering all of our experience helping people discover and utilize their individual learning styles, we're quite sensitive to the role of environmental influences on the learning process. Judging by a number of personal experiences, not all facilitators share the awareness of how the training venue can affect a participant's mood and ability to learn. We make certain the facilities we use are bright, roomy, and aesthetically pleasing. Several years ago, the two of us attended a week-long training program that proved exceedingly uncomfortable for Pat due to both the venue and the choice of activities.

Pat: Craig and I had heard great things about this particular training program and had reviewed some of the materials, which were excellent. We thought we could utilize some of the concepts in our own team programs. Although it's a stretch for me to think about an entire week out of the office because of all the details that need my attention, I decided that gaining certification in this particular program would be worth the effort. As it turned out, everything about the facility, the facilitation, and the program setup was totally wrong for my temperament and learning style.

First of all, it was the middle of February—the most depressing month for me due to short days and lack of sunlight. Secondly, the venue was a basement room with cinderblock walls, no natural light, and very little heat. The rectangular fake wood tables and metal folding chairs did nothing to enhance the bleak surroundings. And worst of all, the focus of the program, which had been billed as team building, turned out to be deep personal exploration and sharing—not something I care to engage in with twenty strangers!

Despite all these negatives, I persevered until the fourth day. That morning, the facilitator broke us into pairs to discuss our innermost feelings about a past personal experience. I reluctantly joined my partner, suggesting he go first (while I desperately searched my memory for an appropriate incident to share). He began relating an emotional encounter with his father and broke down sobbing. I'm a sympathetic person, but I couldn't imagine sharing that level of emotion with a total stranger. Plus, I had no idea how such an activity was relevant to facilitating a professional team building program! I bailed out at lunchtime and never returned. Poor Craig was left to explain my disappearance to the rest of the group! I still cringe at the thought of that experience.

Craig learned very early in his career how to handle unexpected challenges related to group facilitation. About six months after he became career planning and placement director, he was asked by a fellow director at a branch campus to give a short talk about hiring recent graduates.

Craig: Seeking more specifics, I asked if the audience would consist of employers interested in hiring graduating students. The answer was yes. I had numerous ideas for the presentation, and as usual, I finalized my thoughts in the car on my way to the meeting. Upon arrival, I discovered that the audience was made up of placement directors from other area colleges, all of whom had been in their positions years longer than me. I also learned that I was scheduled to be onstage for two hours. As usual, I was energized rather than dismayed at this unexpected challenge. I discarded my original plan and transformed the presentation into group facilitation on the topic of how to help place students in a difficult economy. Fortunately, the participants had many creative ideas and were delighted to share their approaches rather than listen to someone talk for two hours.

The many curveballs we have encountered while planning and facilitating programs have caused varying degrees of concern, not only on our part. During a leadership retreat, the person hired to direct an orienteering activity didn't show up at the appointed time. Doug had facilitated this energizing segment of the program for several years, and we knew him to be very reliable. Craig was concerned that something serious had happened to him while the program director, experiencing her first retreat, was panicked because she feared the program would be ruined. Being new to her job, she had no knowledge of Craig's talent of adjusting seamlessly to unexpected situations. He substituted a challenging activity in place of orienteering that served the same purpose, and the retreat continued without a hitch. We later learned that Doug was fine and had simply recorded the date in his calendar incorrectly.

On another occasion, it was the program facility that presented the surprise. A San Diego-based company asked us to plan and lead a three-day program for their management team. They also requested a ropes course challenge as part of the agenda. Being unfamiliar with the area or the availability of ropes facilities, we asked the HR director to locate a venue and book local facilitators to lead the ropes challenge the first day of the program. We agreed to design and direct the following two days of programming. A few days later, our contact let us know that she had hired two trainers formerly with the Tony Robbins organization to lead the ropes course activities. We looked forward to interacting with them and observing their approach and techniques.

Pat: Craig and I flew to San Diego the day before the program and drove up the coast the following morning. The facility, about an hour north of San Diego, was absolutely beautiful. We met the two ropes course facilitators and found them interesting, energetic, and fun. However, there was one problem—the HR person had neglected to make the precise inquiry when booking the facility. There was no ropes course! Ned and Jim were trained specifically for ropes course facilitation and couldn't offer alternative programming, so they left. In place of that segment, Craig devised a challenging activity on the spur of the moment—one that echoed the company's work system. The afternoon proved to be quite productive as the team used the experience and subsequent discussion to devise ways of improving their existing work process. The remaining two days went as planned, leaving our client pleased with the outcome and grateful for Craig's ability to adapt so effectively.

You never know where the curveball might come from. The venue, the participants, or even Mother Nature can cause disruptions. Craig was facilitating a two-day outdoor adventure program at a remote facility for the managers of a major power company when the unexpected happened.

Craig: We had just about completed the first day of the program when I saw several people suddenly grab their cell phones, listen briefly, and take off running toward their cars. An electrical storm had hit the city, which was about forty-five minutes from the camp, and the entire group disappeared in a matter of minutes to deal with the power outages. I was truly impressed at the speed with which they departed! It was the only time I was ever abandoned by an entire group in the middle of a program. We rescheduled the second day of the program for a later date and finished without interruption.

The same company contacted me a few months later to conduct a program for their department managers. Initially, they requested a team building program. As I worked with the leader to design the process, I discovered that the company's reward system placed individuals in competition with each other to the point of receiving personal "report cards" that rated their effectiveness. I suggested that this group really couldn't qualify as a team, and that participating in team activities was apt to create more harm than good. So the program was designed and delivered as a group outing with individual and group challenges.

Management is sometimes blind to the fact that team building simply is not appropriate for groups that, like the one described above, operate in a competitive environment. An individual once told us about his organization's approach to year-end bonuses. Each employee gets a yearly evaluation, and based on their score, people are divided into three equal groups. Those in the top third get a bonus. Those in the middle third don't get a bonus. And money is *deducted* from those in the bottom third to pay the bonuses of the top third! Yet those company officials claim to want people to work together as a team.

Such stories explain why we take lots of time to discuss company culture and structure before we agree to conduct a team program. Even taking that precaution, we don't always find out about issues that significantly affect a group's ability to function as a team until we are in the middle of the process. That's one of the key reasons we developed our team survey to gather data from program participants. The survey has saved us more than once from embarking on a program that could have been more harmful than helpful.

The director of an educational organization asked us to conduct a program for his group. He explained that there was a lot of anger among staff members and claimed he didn't know the cause of their discontent. We urged him to include the TAS as part of the process to help pinpoint specific problems. The responses to the survey were sobering. Participants indicated that there had been some incidences of sexual harassment among staff members. Craig shared the information with the director and told him that the harassment issue must be dealt with before he would facilitate a team program. The director was not pleased, but Craig convinced him that a team program would be a waste of time and money and could be more harmful than helpful under such circumstances.

Just when we think we've seen everything, another eye-opening experience proves that there is no end to the surprises. A city government asked Craig to conduct a program for their mediation team on the subject of group facilitation and consensus building skills. These folks go out into neighborhoods and facilitate group meetings in the attempt to find mutually satisfactory solutions to neighborhood disputes.

Craig: I usually begin this type of a program with a discussion about worst-case scenarios. Once people determine ways to work through those issues, the rest is easy. This group had participants with varying degrees of experience, so I asked individuals to share stories about the biggest barrier to group consensus they had encountered. One man shared that his worst experience in a session was when he discovered that one participant was armed! That immediately put me out of my realm of experience. I told the group that I wasn't going to pretend to have an answer for that situation and asked if anyone else had had the same experience (one other person had). So I requested that those two people share how they had responded and then invited the entire group to brainstorm additional options and think about how they might handle a similar situation. After that discussion, we worked through many less serious scenarios. The session proved to be very valuable to everyone, including me!

Another surprise that required some adjustment to the original plan occurred when Craig was about leave the house to conduct a day-long team building program for an arts organization. While having breakfast, he scanned the newspaper. He noticed a brief item on the front page mentioning that the organization he was about to meet with was undergoing significant changes in leadership. The article didn't go into any detail, and Craig had no idea whether the program would go on as scheduled, whether the employees had been told of the changes in advance, or just what was in store. He arrived at the venue to find the whole team, along with a few board members, awaiting his arrival. A board member informed the group that the director of the organization—the person who had hired Craig—had resigned the day before. The board members determined that the program should proceed even in light of this startling news. Without missing a beat, Craig changed gears and conducted a program that focused on working together in times of change, offering the employees some of the skills they would need to help them through the next few months.

Craig: A spur of the moment adjustment also was required when I worked with a group of managers from a federal government agency. After just a short time working with them, I found that whenever an important issue was raised, it was met with silence rather than discussion. It was clear the group saw me as an outsider. I surmised from their personality profiles and from the fact that they worked with highly confidential information that they were not comfortable discussing certain sensitive issues while I was in the room. So for some segments of the program, I posed an issue for them to discuss, gave them specific questions to answer, set a timetable, and then left the room. I observed them occasionally through the glass door and saw that the level of interaction was quite lively when I wasn't present. When they completed discussing a topic, they called me back to continue the facilitation. It was one of my stranger programs, but I adjusted to their needs to the best of my ability, and they were pleased with the outcome.

An odd revelation came to light when we worked with the employees of a private insurance company. Throughout the program, the participants were very reserved and extremely proper. They were also highly engaged in the process and generated excellent insights and discussions. We asked them to consider how they might make some significant forward-thinking changes in the way the office was run based on some of the things they had learned about their operating styles during the program. After a bit of hesitation, one young woman summoned up the courage to suggest that they might consider turning off the bells. Upon further questioning, we learned that bells rang at the beginning of the workday, at the beginning and end of breaks, and before and after lunch. The bells indicated the times that all administrative staff had to be seated at their desks! It took us a minute to process what had just been said. After all, it was the 1990s, not the 1890s! There was actually a lengthy and serious discussion about the pros and cons of making such an "earth-shaking" decision. Fortunately, management decided that this was a change they were willing to make! Everyone seemed delighted that they had taken such an important step forward, and we were once again reminded that every organization exists in its own reality.

One of our common practices is to adapt all program activities and materials to reflect the nature of our client's business. When working with a group in the health care field, we decided our warm-up activity would be a mute lineup based on pulse rate. Without talking, the participants were asked to form a line in order of each individual's pulse rate, starting with the lowest rate and ending with the highest. They had to accomplish the task without speaking. Our reasoning in choosing that activity turned out to be slightly flawed because the participants were administrators of a health care association, not actual health care workers. We were still surprised that some of them didn't know exactly how to take their own pulse. That activity was less than successful and perhaps a bit embarrassing for some members of the group. We made a few minor adjustments in our program agenda, and the remainder of the day went smoothly.

A health emergency was responsible for a major curve thrown at Craig as he prepared to facilitate a retreat for the executive team of a large media organization. He and the company vice president had spent weeks discussing goals and outcomes and designing a rather complex three-day program. Just days before the program, Craig received word that the vice president had had not one, but two major heart attacks.

Craig: This was a high profile, highly stressed, and extremely driven organization. Joe and I had spent many hours on the phone planning the three-day program for the executive team. The agenda was very ambitious,

including "supposedly brief" reports from each team member about his or her specific area of responsibility in addition to the team activities and discussions I was to facilitate. I had everything prepared for the event when I got word from Joe's assistant that Joe was in the hospital. When he was able to talk on the phone, I heard from Joe himself. He insisted the program proceed without him but with a very different focus.

Joe was obviously shaken by his brush with death. He wanted to change the whole focus of the retreat from an emphasis on work to an emphasis on healthy living. He urged his team to bring their families to the retreat and even for family members to participate in the work sessions, which would now focus on relationships and healthy living. He asked that the menu be changed to emphasize healthy eating habits and urged participants turn off cell phones and beepers while they were at the retreat. He also hoped they would stay beyond the planned events and enjoy the beautiful setting with their families rather than rush back to the office.

I changed my portion of the program according to Joe's wishes. In the original agenda, in addition to team activities, each team member was to make a presentation about their particular department—their accomplishments for the past year and their plans for the year to come. But now Joe wanted those presentations shortened so I could lead them in more group activities to enhance camaraderie and help them provide support to each other. That didn't happen! Joe's second in command took over in his absence, and the retreat became the scene of "who can grab the most airtime." When they weren't listening to each other's interminable Power Point presentations, most folks were on their cell phones checking in at the office. They showed little interest in the few team challenges I had the opportunity to introduce or even in group discussions about ways to enhance their effectiveness. And just about everyone drove straight to the office when the retreat ended. It was clear that their leader's epiphany had no effect on the others.

For us, the most disturbing surprises are those that are actual setups. We're very straightforward people and have trouble understanding why anyone would spend the time and money to plan a corporate program with every intention of sabotaging the process. But it has happened to us a few times. Craig is great at handling the unexpected, but even he can be blindsided by sabotage since it's just not on his radar screen.

We had completed several departmental programs for a large hospital system when we were asked to design and facilitate a two-day retreat for the

entire management team and the department heads from all of the hos
There were about forty people involved and they chose to meet at a
park. The program included exploring group and individual operat
styles, outdoor challenges, and indoor group discussions on ways to impro
organizational processes both departmentally and hospital-wide.

*Pat: We noticed what we considered to be an undercurrent of hostility from
the very beginning. We often have beach balls and hula hoops and various
other toys around the room at the beginning of programs as we wait for
everyone to arrive. Some people choose to talk or sit quietly while others
need activity. Several of the males in this group chose to toss around some
beach balls. Within a couple minutes, the harmless activity escalated into
actually spiking balls at each other volleyball style, and we wondered to
ourselves what caused such aggressive behavior.*

*The program proceeded according to plan, and the team seemed to be
gaining energy and insights. On the afternoon of the second day, we were
all in a conference room discussing the team's progress and determining
how they might apply what they had learned in order to make positive
changes in their business operations. We noticed that the CEO had been
silent throughout the discussion. He was stretched out in his chair with his
arms behind his head, his legs fully extended, and a bemused look on his
face. Finally, he stood up and said, "I think you're all a bunch of slackers!"
Then turning to us, he said, "Now let's see you facilitate that!" Craig quite
coolly answered, "That issue doesn't fit with the purpose or agenda of this
program, but if you would like to facilitate such a discussion, please go
right ahead." Thankfully, that silenced the CEO, and it also gave us insight
into what might have caused the aggressive behavior that the group had
exhibited earlier. We continued the program, but clearly, that incident
had an effect on the participants and on us as well. In subsequent years,
after the retirement of the CEO, we had a wonderful working relationship
with that organization.*

Second only to the competence of the facilitator, the success of a program
hinges directly on the level of commitment of the highest-ranking individual
in attendance. So, if at all possible, we try to interact with that person during
the planning process. She or he doesn't need to be actively involved in the
planning, but should approve the agenda and participate actively with the
team during the actual retreat. We've dealt with many wonderful CEOs,
presidents, and department managers who have fully supported the team

concept and the process of enhancing it. We've also encountered those, like the CEO we just mentioned, who show no interest or, worse yet, actively or passively sabotage the process.

After our outstanding experience with the local county court system, which we described earlier, we were asked by another court system to deliver a similar program. We brought in the former presiding judge (who was now retired) from the first program to be part of our consulting team. We primarily interacted with the court administrator during the planning process. The design of the program called for us to interview selected judges and employees prior to the program to determine what issues they considered most important. The data we gathered, plus the results of the TAS, indicated that there were numerous communication issues, discontent with the treatment of individuals within the system and little sense of harmony within the team.

After extensive interviews and careful preparation, we anticipated the retreat with high hopes. Those hopes were not realized. The first stumbling block was that, despite our advice to go off-site, the retreat was held at the court building on a Saturday. It is much more beneficial to get people away from their familiar surroundings in order to expand their thinking. A different setting stimulates more creativity and, most importantly, changes the way people relate to each other. Even though we weren't pleased with the venue, we still felt we would be able to reach the goals we had developed.

Pat: It was the administrative judge who set the stage for an ineffective session. He arrived with his newspaper and spent the entire day either reading or working puzzles as the retreat unfolded around him. He never took part in any discussion or activity and seldom raised his eyes from the paper. None of the three of us consultants was comfortable confronting him. The rest of the group was apparently used to his passive-aggressive behavior and largely ignored him. But it was very distracting, especially because we knew that without his buy-in, or interest, in improving the organization, the impact of the retreat would be limited. When we followed up with the court administrator several months later, he reported a significant improvement in the way the team members interacted, but noted that much of their enthusiasm was diminished because there had been little change in attitude among the judges.

Craig: I experienced a similar outcome working with a large food distributor in the south. I conducted a general team program with the entire employee group and worked quite extensively with the management team. The managers really wanted to see the company thrive and spent lots of time discussing ways to improve their functions and processes. I also met with each manager one on one to help them enhance their individual contributions, set goals, and develop specific plans for moving forward.

My goal was to meet with each person during every trip, but despite careful advance scheduling, managers were often unavailable because they were assigned to last-minute tasks. I began to doubt the level of commitment by the top executives despite the fact that they had been the ones who requested my help. My intuition proved to be correct. In the final analysis, most of the ideas generated by the management team were ignored or rejected and the company continued to operate as it always had. I know the lack of progress was as frustrating for many of the participants as it was for me. One day, as I was leaving their facility, I was asked by one of the executives when I would be back again. My frustration was evident as I replied, "Never! You're wasting your money and my time." I explained that, in my opinion, the team would be better off if the executives just continued issuing orders rather than asking for ideas and suggestions that were totally disregarded. He was surprised at my candor and that I would turn down additional work.

As open and straightforward as we are, we occasionally find ourselves lightning rods for people with hidden agendas. We were asked to meet with Joyce the human resources director of a small manufacturing operation to discuss some management development programming. She indicated that the company was instituting a series of development initiatives and were very interested in using Craig to develop and deliver them. After several discussions, Joyce asked Craig to plan and facilitate a sample program while she observed, indicating that it was simply a formality prior to closing the deal.

Craig: The initial assignment was to work with a group of managers to help them develop ways to encourage brainstorming and gain group consensus among their employees. I suggested using nominal group technique as an easy and consistent way to gain consensus. Joyce liked that idea, and we agreed to go forward. I was totally unaware of Joyce's hidden agenda. She sat in on the session and essentially sabotaged everything I did. She went so far as to heckle me with comments like, "It would certainly be helpful if I could see the flip chart!" and "What is this nominal group process, some $100 term?" I never encountered such rudeness either before or after that session. We later discovered the reason behind her behavior. Joyce had *already decided on the person she wanted to hire for the programs, but she had been directed by her boss to try out at least one other facilitator before she made a final decision. Although it helped to learn the reason behind the treatment I received, it didn't erase the memory of a terrible experience.*

Rather than dwelling on the negatives, we prefer recalling some of the unexpected experiences that surpassed our expectations. Groups that have fun together can accomplish wonderful things. Frequently, when we facilitate two- or three-day programs, our clients ask for additional group activities in the evening just for fun. One favorite activity calls for teams to earn points by doing silly tricks, telling jokes, and sharing special talents. The teams assume they are competing with each other but gradually discover that they can earn more points by cooperating among themselves. This activity has produced many memorable moments including: a nun who told an off-color joke to earn points; a woman who displayed her ability to stick her entire fist into her mouth (only after she made her fellow employees promise not to tell her husband that she displayed this talent); and a participant who brought the chair, lamp, coffee table, and various other items from his room as props for his skit!

We also enjoy tailoring activities to fit the industry or special focus of each group. When working with a company that provides building supplies, we used an activity called the Nail Balance. We broke them into small groups of four or five people with the challenge of balancing as many half-penny nails as possible on top of one nail that is driven into a block of wood. We hadn't anticipated that they would become so engrossed in the effort and have so much fun trying to figure out the "secret." (The record number of nails that can be balanced is said to be in the eighties.) Even now, several years after their retreat, the participants mention that activity whenever we meet.

Overall, we've been able to adapt pretty readily to the unexpected by adjusting to unforeseen circumstances, learning from difficult moments, letting go of things out of our control, and enjoying the pleasant surprises. The secret is lots of experience, flexibility, and a large repertoire of meaningful activities. Here are some additional tips.

How to prepare for the unexpected

- Work with the person at the highest appropriate level to clarify and commit to realistic goals and deliverables.

- If challenged during a program, direct the attention back to the individual or group by asking, "How might *you* handle that?" or "How would *you* like to proceed?"
- Always have a plan B such as additional activities, discussion ideas, etc.
- Carefully check out the facility *before* the program. Pay special attention to the training room you'll be using and the noise level you might expect. (And watch out for those bow hunters!)
- If possible and appropriate, use an up-front survey to gather information about the team or group. We are amazed by the information people reveal when completing our TAS.
- If you are using a survey or conducting interviews, make absolutely sure you NEVER divulge any information that has been given to you in confidence. Much of our effectiveness is a result of the level of trust we establish with our clients.
- Plan activities that relate to the group's business focus and the way they operate.
- Adjust to the group as the program progresses.
- Don't be averse to taking time out during a program to regroup or clarify goals. In the rare situations where continuing the program could be damaging, there is always the option of interrupting or even rescheduling the program.

CHAPTER 8

Success Factors and Shortfalls

Embracing the advice to "do what you love," we periodically review our own progress, evaluate our level of satisfaction, and make adjustments to the assignments we accept and our approach to those assignments. Our goal is to keep the best and drop the rest. Recently, we decided to take a more systematic and thorough approach to that evaluation procedure.

Craig assembled a group of former clients who had experienced one or more of our programs or consulting processes. A fellow consultant facilitated a discussion about our organization's strengths and weaknesses and led the group in brainstorming ways we could capitalize on those strengths as we contemplate the future. In preparation for that exercise, we asked randomly selected clients to respond to the following questions about the services we provided to their organizations: (1) what did the Rider Group bring to the process that no one else could have offered, and (2) what primary value/benefit did our services provide to your organization. The responses revealed that our clients appreciate the *style* of our approach and delivery as much as the content of our programming.

In general most of our clients are enthused about the fact that we *partner* with their organizations rather than operating as an outside expert who "has all the answers." This style of consulting enables an organization to determine solutions to *their own* unique issues. In our minds, every organization is different; and while there are certain effective business practices, the application of those practices varies with the personality of each specific group. Our main goal has always been to help individuals and organizations make the best use of unique strengths and talents they already possess and to

140

help them develop in areas where they can improve. Although that approach requires designing a unique process for each client group, the results are well worth the extra effort.

Craig: I'm not an expert in every client's type of business. My approach is to provide individuals or groups with the tools they need and to show them how to apply those tools to produce the desired results. Whether using the MBTI, the LPI, or our own TAS, the goal is to strengthen an organization by helping team members appreciate their individual and collective strengths and minimize any weaknesses. We merely help people discover and utilize the power they already possess.

The second question we asked our clients was about the value the Rider Group brought to their organization. Respondents state that we make it possible for each individual to shine and encourage the collective group to respect individual differences. "No one can create self-awareness and build teams better or faster," says one corporate executive. Our commitment to helping individuals with diverse backgrounds and talents respect their differences is a main factor that sets us apart from many consultants. We believe that once individuals and teams learn that kind of respect for each other, they can achieve almost any goal they decide to pursue.

Armed with feedback from our clients, we began reviewing the outcomes of our work over time. Careful evaluation of our successes and shortfalls provides much-needed insight as we chart our future. We highly recommend such a process for everyone, no matter what business you're in or what role you fill.

As we reflect on past accomplishments and challenges, it becomes clear that some outcomes are the result of conscious design—some are due to our natural preferences, and some are pure happenstance. What follows are factors (both positive and negative) that have been most important in shaping our business journey. We consider them to be important considerations for other individuals and organizations as well.

SUCCESS FACTORS

Location, location, location: Your location can be a vital element in meeting your personal and professional needs and goals. Special considerations include the size of the community, its amenities for you and your family, and the ease of becoming involved and visible.

This advice is especially relevant to establishing a small business. Important factors include market size, proximity of goods and services your company requires, labor force issues, your target clientele, transportation, communication, and a host of other issues. Although the electronic age has diminished the importance of some of these considerations, each business and industry comes with its own set of imperatives.

We were fortunate to reside in a community that was ideal for starting and sustaining a small business. In 1979, the population of the Dayton metropolitan area was approximately two hundred fifty thousand people. It was small enough for us to get involved in important community activities and to make a name for ourselves quickly yet large enough to provide exceptional business opportunities. Building a positive reputation is especially important when establishing a business with a specialty as personal as career development and outplacement. We had to assure our clients—both the organizations that hired us and the individuals who were the direct recipients of our services—that they could trust both our confidentiality and our competence. That task was made easier because of Craig's visibility as director of career planning and placement at a university and Pat's position with a well-known public accounting firm.

Dayton is known as a cradle of invention and technology and was a thriving mecca for manufacturing companies through the 1970s. The area's rich legacy of innovation and craftsmanship played an important role in the evolution of the automotive industry and other important enterprises. Dayton resident Charles Kettering invented the self-starter for the automobile while other well-known inventors and industrialists, including the Wright Brothers, were responsible for the large numbers of factories and corporate headquarters in the city, many of which became valued clients over the years.

In the late 1970s and throughout the next decade, the manufacturing sector began its downward slide—a phenomenon that gave us our start in the outplacement business. Word traveled fast in Dayton's "small town" environment, and our business thrived with little need for formal marketing. A few years later, as we ventured into team development and retreat facilitation, the majority of our business was with the large corporations and service industries headquartered in the Dayton area. Our working relationships with these companies gave us the opportunity to travel to numerous subsidiaries and branch locations throughout the country, and our reputation spread much further than just the local community. Word of mouth continues to serve us well, and individuals who leave local companies and move elsewhere often contact us to provide programs at their new locations.

The impressive history of entrepreneurship in this community still survives despite the large downsizings and the gradual disappearance of manufacturing businesses. There are still plenty of organizations—large and small—to support businesses like ours. Added into the mix are several hospitals and health care facilities, a mix of high-tech organizations, multiple universities, and Wright-Patterson Air Force Base—one of the largest employers in the state.

Because of the midrange size of the community, it's easy to get involved. We believe strongly that it is important to give back to the community that sustains us. Early in our business venture, we became actively involved in the chamber of commerce with Craig serving on its board. Each of us has served on several not-for-profit boards. Pat's volunteer work has been so extensive that she has received two prestigious community awards. We have always discounted our services for the not-for-profit sector and donate time, energy, and money for many worthy local causes.

Partially because of our involvement in the community and our contributions of time and money to nonprofit organizations, we have never had to market our services in conventional ways. Instead, we focus on building solid relationships and maintaining our reputation for providing more than is expected. Our business is a prime example that "the more you give, the more you get back," and we are grateful to be in a community that has supported us for more than twenty years.

Focus on the customer: A second success factor is the *way* the work is accomplished. Our approach is to serve client companies by focusing on the uniqueness of each individual, each team, and each organization. That philosophy helps individuals recognize their own strengths while encouraging the entire team to value both individual contributions and the collective power of the team. Our approach emerged naturally from our initial work in the outplacement business. Most of our individual clients have been very competent people whose talents went unrecognized or underutilized in their organizations. Once they realized their potential, they went on to do great things and often turned to us for help building their own teams in the organizations they joined. Our natural curiosity about people and their talents and our ability to work with all types at all levels of an organization are characteristics that have set us apart from many other consultants, thus limiting our need for conventional marketing.

Problem solving: No matter what your field of work, it's important to see yourself as a problem solver. Once our clients realize that we are willing to try to resolve almost *any* problem they encounter in the area of employee relations, there are no limits to the variety of requests we receive. During the peak of the outplacement frenzy, we suggested every creative idea imaginable to help a company retain an employee. Occasionally, we were able to help them adapt job descriptions or adjust work hours and responsibilities in ways that made it possible to avoid dismissing key employees. Consequently, there are folks who have never forgotten our efforts, and it's common for us to run into people who remember us from an interaction that occurred fifteen or twenty years ago.

Craig: We had established a reputation for problem solving and welcomed challenges that others would not even consider accepting. A university approached us to handle the outplacement of one of their employees with special needs. Mike was bright, extremely competent, and an excellent writer, and he had cerebral palsy. The first thing we did as we began to work together was to look for organizations where Mike's perceived handicap was actually an asset. After careful investigation, we found that the federal government had a special program focused on hiring individuals with perceived disabilities. We contacted a colleague at the air force base who provided us with a list of job openings, and Mike targeted his search efforts on those opportunities. He soon accepted an offer there even though the position was not at the level of his capabilities. Within a very short period of time, Mike had proven his competence and was promoted to what he describes as his dream job.

Adaptability: In our minds, another key requirement for success is the ability to adapt to change. The rate of change in the current business and cultural climate continues to accelerate exponentially. What has helped us keep up with the pace of change is the knowledge of our core strengths. With such awareness, we are able to design and adapt our business in ways that allow each of us to spend the majority of our time doing what we love. Over the years, this flexibility has enabled us to adjust to personal needs (such as family), develop new interests and expertise that are in demand and react to monumental changes in the general business environment. We even alternated the role of company president (and changed the sign on the door) every two years to emphasize the fact that we are *equal* partners.

It's important to us to stay ahead of the curve as changes occur in trends and approaches, but not fall prey to the "program du jour." We've been willing to let go of major tools and processes we have used for years—even those that were still extremely popular—when we see they no longer accomplish the appropriate goals. One example is the use of ropes courses. We utilized them extensively for team building programs in the late '80s and early '90s but eventually realized their limitations for achieving desired results for our clients. We observed that ropes courses, especially the high ropes, favor male participants since success with some activities requires upper body strength and taller stature. We determined that it could harm rather than enhance team development when some percentage of the team starts off at a disadvantage. In response to that realization, we designed and implemented activities that don't require specific physical strengths or abilities but *do* keep everyone actively engaged and on a level playing field.

The use of assessment tools is another area where we adjusted our approach, primarily due to time constraints. Years ago, we used a process called the Personal Strength Inventory (PSI), which involved individual interviews and personal feedback with each program participant. It was very enlightening for individuals and the team to understand their collective strengths and abilities. It also provided a wealth of information that we could use in designing group programs. However, due to the time involved in gathering and processing that information, the PSI isn't feasible in today's work environment, and we only utilize it in very specific situations.

In the past few years, some of our clients have even shunned the use of the MBTI because of the time it takes to appropriately process the information. Our belief in the importance of some type of framework for understanding and valuing the talents of each team member has led us to substitute other less time-consuming methods of demonstrating differences. For Craig, adaptability is second nature, so these changes have been easy for him to make. As demonstrated by many of the stories in preceding chapters, he is constantly trying out new ways to help people grasp and retain concepts. Sometimes he alters his plans for other reasons, such as making a point to those who brazenly resist program guidelines.

Craig: Many programs I facilitate include an overnight stay at a lodge or conference center. I'm very precise about the schedule for each program, especially the starting time for the second morning. If breakfast is part of the package, I make sure participants know that they need to finish eating before they come to the training room. Lately, it has become a more common occurrence for a few independent (or passive-aggressive) souls to bring their breakfast with them with the intention of eating during the program despite the fact that it is both rude and distracting. In these cases, I adapt my schedule and begin with an "up and around" activity for the group, forcing the scofflaws to leave their breakfast on the table to grow cold. It's a subtle way of reinforcing the message that inconsiderate behavior negatively affects not just the facilitator but the other attendees who are participating in an activity.

As a program progresses, we occasionally observe other incidences or behaviors that require adjustments. Sometimes a group reacts differently than we had anticipated to a particular activity or format. In that case, we change the activity and try a new approach until we bring the group to where they need to be. It takes experience and practice to combine the art of reading people's needs with the science of program development.

Craig: In the course of working with a management team, I used an activity requiring participants to "unscramble" letters to correctly spell the names of major cities. As usually happens, people considered this an individual challenge rather than a group activity to the point of shielding their answers from others at the table. Some people finished quickly while others took much longer. At the conclusion of the activity, I led a discussion during which the group acknowledged that the exercise had not been presented as an individual task. Participants agreed that they would have been more successful had they combined their talents.

As the program proceeded, I gave them a second challenge. Again, they chose to work alone with similar results. They still hadn't internalized the benefits of sharing their knowledge. Finally, after a third frustrating situation, the participants initiated a lengthy conversation comparing the way they operate at work with the activities they had just completed. Determined to enhance their effectiveness by pooling their talents and problem solving skills, they developed some ground rules they pledged to use at work.

While developing that program, I had not anticipated that it would take three activities and considerable discussion time to bring about the desired result. Obviously, I had to adjust other elements of the program to stay on schedule. Had I not been willing to adapt my agenda, the organization may never have achieved the breakthrough that significantly enhanced their effectiveness at work.

Niche Markets: Another key to success in the consulting arena is to target specific markets that match your areas of skill and expertise. It's much easier to sell and deliver a project or program when you don't have to keep reinventing yourself. Our focus on maximizing our own individual talents resulted in the development of some interesting and lucrative niche markets for us.

Craig thrives on unscripted facilitation and that is truly his specialty. But Pat doesn't necessarily enjoy the free-flowing processes demanded by our team building programs. Even though she sees the positive results of such programs and *can* fill that role when necessary, it just isn't as fun and rewarding for her as we believe work should be. Consequently, over the years, we developed other specialty business to take advantage of Pat's special talents.

Pat: I am quite comfortable facilitating a group if it involves a defined, predictable, and controlled process. One area where my talents flourish is focus group facilitation. In this arena, it is crucial to develop the appropriate questions, ask them in exactly the same way to each person or group that is interviewed, provide a trusting environment, and gather data in a consistent manner. It's a group process that suits my methodical style and one that I truly enjoy. I even enjoy compiling and analyzing the data and developing a compelling presentation of the results—tasks that are especially unappealing to Craig.

One particularly interesting focus group project involved a large hospital system seeking input from a cross section of employees on how they viewed their work environment, what they considered problem areas, and what improvements they might suggest. From what we observed in other organizations, it was unusual for organizations—especially ones who were thriving—to seek extensive employee input. Initially, I was a bit suspicious of management's motives and wary of gathering information that might be used improperly. But after spending several planning sessions with the human resources director and the vice president, I became convinced of their sincere desire to discover what employees were thinking in order to continue making positive changes. Together, we designed a process in which the confidentiality of all comments and data was carefully protected.

Questionnaires were sent to employees from all levels, departments, and specialty areas. Individuals were then selected randomly to participate in focus groups. I personally conducted all of the focus groups—at all times of the day and night to accommodate different shifts—and compiled the data from both the survey and the focus groups. The data was presented to the HR professionals, and together we brainstormed solutions to address employee concerns and developed a plan for implementing specific changes.

We repeated the process two years later to see if employees were satisfied with the changes that had been made. I shared those results with the executive officers and board members, who were delighted to find that employee satisfaction and productivity had increased significantly. The entire project was a great match for my style because it was straightforward, there was a very concrete product, I could see the results of my efforts, and there were no surprises!

Pat also enjoyed designing and directing community leadership programs. Those programs introduce participants to the strengths, weaknesses, and inner workings of all the systems in a community or region. We first facilitated the opening retreat of a citywide leadership program in 1988. In 1994, Pat took on the directorship of that program for the chamber of commerce. Soon thereafter, the chamber asked us to help design and to direct a regional leadership program and an introductory program for corporate CEOs and executive officers new to the community. A few years later, Pat became director of the statewide leadership program as well.

The requirements of designing and running leadership programs were a great match for Pat's organizational and logistical skills and her desire to create a positive learning environment. Her efforts were recognized by both state and international awards. These leadership programs also provided us with a forum to showcase our expertise in group facilitation, which resulted in the opportunity to work with many of the companies represented in the leadership programs. Craig still facilitates the opening retreats for all of these programs as well as several similar programs in other states. That visibility has gained us many clients over the years.

Sharing talents and expertise: Part of the enjoyment of having a successful business is the attention you attract. We often get requests to tell our story, and we willingly share our talents and knowledge with others. An important factor in the success of our business is that we share our divergent perspectives with each other. Even when we work separately on programs or projects, we review our agendas and processes together. Each of us has strengths and blind spots, and sharing our viewpoints helps us prepare for all contingencies.

Pat: One of the ways I can be helpful to Craig is by helping him develop instructions for some of the activities he includes in his programming. I am a very step-by-step learner (a sensor in MBTI terms) as is approximately

75 percent of the general population. Craig is an intuitive, and when it comes to giving directions, he can be a bit too nonspecific for us sensors. We illustrate this contrast in our styles by sharing how differently we prepare for a trip. My preparation is detailed and precise. I used to request the trip ticks from AAA; now I go to Google or MapQuest for detailed information. So I was astounded to learn that, in his younger days, Craig embarked on a trip from New York to Colorado with only one piece of information—take Interstate 80 to Nebraska and turn left (and he didn't have any idea how to get to Interstate 80)! You can imagine that such imprecise directions might leave some of our program participants puzzled as to what is expected of them!

Craig: My contribution to Pat is to help her see the big picture when she gets mired down in the details. She may concentrate on getting each specific point across to a group and neglect to tie the information together with an overarching concept or purpose. We have learned from experience that discussing our program plans and agendas together significantly improves the final product.

We liberally share our skills and expertise with others as well. Former program participants often contact us to get advice about using one of our program activities within their organizations. Many of these requests come from educational and not-for-profit entities that cannot afford to hire us to facilitate numerous programs. We accommodate those requests even though we're essentially giving away our bread and butter. Once in a while, someone takes advantage of our good nature and uses one of our ideas for their own profit. When that happens, we remind ourselves that "imitation is the most sincere form of flattery"!

Creativity: Part of the advantage of running your own business is the ability to reinvent yourself whenever you see a new opportunity. We have adapted to monumental changes in the workplace and haven't been afraid to venture into uncharted territory. This clear pattern has emerged as we adjusted our business focus from career development to outplacement and then to team building, coaching, and training facilitators. Even within those specialty areas, no two programs we develop or deliver are ever identical. When the content *is* similar, we adapt the details to each organization's particular focus and goals. That boosts our own level of interest as well as serving the client more effectively.

Craig: Our approach has always been to customize each program or process specifically to individual clients. That keeps our programming fresh and as interesting for us as it is for our clients. Recently, I learned that a client was planning a trip to reward their sales team members for excellent results. The vice president wanted something more unique than the standard golfing and dining activities and contacted me to see if I had any ideas. I suggested they spend a few days in Hilton Head, where they could golf, bike, play tennis, sightsee, AND sail on the Stars and Stripes—*a sixty-six-foot sailboat that is docked at Harbor Town. (It was a trial horse for the winner of the 1987 America's Cup race.) The client was interested and commented that everyone would enjoy a relaxing sail on an historic ship, but I had a much different idea in mind. With the approval of the VP, I arranged for the team to actually serve as crew members and learn how to sail the ship. Most of them had no idea how difficult it is to sail a boat—especially a boat of that size—until they actually tried it. After some initial trepidation, almost everyone had a great time, and it was an experience they won't soon forget.*

Fun translates into value: You can't overestimate the value of enjoying your work. We promised ourselves at the start of our business journey that we would never accept an assignment that wasn't both valuable to the client *and* interesting for us. We've been true to that promise to the best of our abilities. Our clients reflect their appreciation for that philosophy. "Valuable AND fun," said one client that we surveyed. "Good humor put people at ease immediately," said another. We are convinced, after years of observation, that a pleasant and lighthearted atmosphere stimulates creativity and learning, making it easier for a group to deal with tough issues.

We recently saw a news clip that indicates the folks at Google—an incredibly successful company—share that philosophy. Google was voted the best place to work by its employees not only because of the many perks they receive but because of the fun and lightheartedness that is encouraged throughout the workday. Employees are emphatic in their belief that such an environment stimulates creativity and innovation. One employee told a reporter that she has so much fun at work it's hard to leave at the end of the day (and then added, with a sheepish look, that she hoped her husband didn't see her interview on television).

Our observations uphold the premise that fun breeds creativity. We've had the pleasure of working with a few very special companies that encouraged a lighthearted approach to work and enjoyed great success as a result. One manufacturer of pet products encouraged its employees to bring their pets to the office. They even had a vice president of animal relations (a golden retriever) who greeted guests in the lobby with an enthusiastic wag of her tail. She would bring her leash to visitors in hopes that they might have time to take her for a stroll outside. Another—a manufacturer of sporting equipment—encouraged its employees to abandon their desks for a certain amount of time each day in favor of wandering around, chatting, and informally brainstorming ideas with each other. Both of those organizations were very successful, had incredibly loyal employees, and received hundreds of resumes from people competing for every job opening. Lately, we have seen few companies encouraging fun and creativity. We hope that the Google publicity sparks new interest in developing such innovative working environments.

Welcome feedback: Another factor that we feel contributes to business success is the desire to receive honest feedback about your work. We continually solicit input from three different groups—participants in our programs, officers and human resource professionals from our client organizations, and other consultants.

At the end of each program, we ask participants to complete evaluation forms with the understanding that we truly want to know how effective the program has been. We've received wonderful comments that make our hard work well worth the effort. We've also received excellent suggestions for improvement and have incorporated numerous changes as a result. And, as expected, there have been some negative comments—often from people who admit that they genuinely dislike group processes. We pay special attention to those comments and try to implement changes that take these opinions into consideration as much as possible, keeping in mind that we will never please all of the people all of the time!

We already mentioned how helpful it was to have a board of advisors who, at a critical time in our company's evolution, assisted us in developing programming relevant to the needs of organizations. We continue to read about new techniques and approaches, listen to organizational concerns regarding employee and team issues, and attend seminars and workshops when we find subjects that are new and exciting. Our goal is to constantly update our programs with new material. Listening to our client groups and the issues that they raise provides some of the most valuable information. We also trade information liberally with other professionals in the field, both informally and through professional organizations. The pace of change in the corporate world demands that programming be constantly updated and improved.

SHORTFALLS

Reviewing your successes is only one half of the evaluation process. We're well aware that there are areas where we have fallen short of our own and others' expectations, and we constantly try to develop and improve. With such a small organization—just the two of us for the last several years—we have had to work especially hard to keep abreast of new technologies and approaches. It's also imperative that we balance the amount of client work we accept in order to have time for professional development opportunities, community service, and just being out and around in the community. We count our disinclination to expand the size and scope of our business among our shortfalls.

Reluctance to add staff: This issue affects us in many ways, including the time we expend on administrative tasks that could be spent with current or potential clients. Part of what holds us back is the memory of our unsuccessful hiring a couple of decades ago. But there are several other reasons—the time it takes to train others, the responsibility for their work product, our perfectionism, and the added pressure of always selling more to cover costs of additional employees. With just the two of us, we are able to select projects based on whether they will be successful, fun, and fulfilling. We are reluctant to lose that flexibility and, in general, have been satisfied with our decision to remain a two-person operation.

Very alone: Besides taking care of all of the administrative details as well as the program development and delivery, the absence of employees means we typically don't have anyone except each other with whom we can brainstorm or share our ideas and enthusiasm. While we respect each others' expertise and opinions, we know each other so well that we feel a need to seek out other perspectives. We have found a few ways to fulfill that need.

Craig is a member of the executive dialogue program, which is sponsored by our city's chamber of commerce. They put together groups of eight to ten executives from different noncompeting business sectors who meet regularly to exchange general business knowledge and give advice and support to each other. Members of a group can raise a specific business topic or problem for discussion—with the assurance that such information is strictly confidential—and receive valuable suggestions and options for addressing the issue. Craig's association with an executive dialogue group has proven very beneficial.

We have also tried teaming up with individuals in our general line of business to share program ideas and even to form alliances on larger pieces of work. That approach has been valuable at times and detrimental at others. In one instance, a fellow consultant chose to "borrow" both our ideas and a client or two. The concept has worked more productively when we engage people in the same line of work but in different geographical areas. We have established several collegial relationships through national professional organizations that have proven to be mutually beneficial.

Blind spots: As indicated by some of the instances we just discussed, both of us tend to take things at face value and to be trustful of others. That occasionally blinds us to the conflicts of interest or the ulterior motives exhibited by some clients as well as some colleagues.

Craig: Years ago, we did a series of Myers-Briggs programs for a large financial institution. It was fun and lucrative work, and both the department managers and staff found the information very useful in improving day-to-day interaction and overall efficiency. In one instance, a manager requested that I work with him and one of his employees in greater depth since they had very different profiles. Unfortunately, the manager seized on their differences as proof that his employee was not suited for the job. I strongly objected and tried to show him how valuable someone with different strengths could be to him and the department. Not only was my advice ignored, but the employee was dismissed, and we were never asked to do another program with that organization.

The outcome was similar when I worked with a department manager in a health care organization. He had received poor evaluations from the folks who reported to him, and I was asked to help him with his interpersonal and management skills. Some factors that contributed to the dissatisfaction were structural and beyond the manager's control, but we addressed as many of the relevant issues as we could. I found him to be willing and anxious to improve and he worked diligently to develop his skills and those of his staff. His scores improved significantly on the next employee evaluation. Nevertheless, shortly thereafter, he was fired. As it turned out, his superiors had no intention of retaining his services, and unbeknownst to me, I had merely been hired to ease the sting of his dismissal. I was as upset as the manager was and let my feelings be known to the person who hired me for the project. Unfortunately, that was the beginning of the end of working with that client.

Firing clients: Occasionally, we fire difficult and/or unreasonable clients or choose not to pursue additional opportunities with them. The director of an organization for which we facilitated an annual two-day retreat began to interfere with the retreat to the extent that it was becoming less and less valuable to the participants. She failed to adhere to the schedule we agreed upon, excused participants from mandatory sessions, and undermined the process to the point that it became less and less effective. When she decided to go out for bids in an effort to reduce an already-generously-discounted fee, we decided that the stress far outweighed the benefits and declined to bid on the work.

Craig: A corporate trainer for a major airline also attempted to take advantage of our desire to please our customers. I presented a program at an international leadership conference on the topic of understanding and working with all types of people. Megan approached me after the program and began to discuss the possibility of my providing training for all the trainers within her organization. As a first step, she asked me to facilitate a similar program for some of the management group so they could evaluate its value. She asked me to significantly discount my fee, assuring me that it would be well worth it in the long run. In addition to a discounted fee, she agreed to provide airfare, expenses for room and board, and reimbursement for materials.

Since my presentation was part of an extensive two-day program under Megan's direction, she was too busy to meet with me at length at the conclusion of my presentation. She indicated that the reviews were excellent, and she would call to discuss future work with the organization. During our conversation a few days later, she asked me to train some trainers who could conduct the program internally, again for the same low fee that I had previously accepted. Although she tried to convince me that this would lead to additional work within the organization, in essence she was asking me to give away my program so that her internal trainers could facilitate it throughout the company. To make matters worse, Megan didn't even live up to her agreement to pay for some of the incidental expenses I had incurred during my initial trip. I realized that I was being treated as a vendor rather than as a valued partner and that this relationship was going nowhere. I declined to pursue it any further.

Everything customized: Earlier in this chapter, we mentioned creativity as one of our strengths, but it also can have a negative effect on our earning potential. We feel it's important to design each program to fit the needs of the organization and the individuals who are participating. That has been a cornerstone of our work. We have watched many fads come and go but refuse to resort to what we refer to as the program du jour. Customizing everything takes more preparation time, and we can't charge much more if we are to remain competitive. We're willing to accept that fact in order to do work we are proud of and enjoy. Our clients end up getting more value for their dollar, although in the current business climate we find that many companies make decisions based solely on cost.

Unpredictable: We have some recurring business we can count on, especially from the community leadership retreats we facilitate and the spin-off work that comes from those programs. Other than that, it is impossible to predict our volume of business from year to year or even from quarter to quarter. That used to make us nervous—and is still disconcerting to our accountant and our financial planner—but we've learned to take it in stride. The fact is that our income has been amazingly consistent from year to year.

Pat: For the past three years, we have had large volumes of work from a few major clients as opposed to our historical experience of one- and two-day programs for a wide variety of clients. While we thought we would enjoy more financial stability with sizeable programs and signed contracts, that didn't prove true. One of our largest clients was very slow to pay, and we didn't have any leverage to insist upon a faster turnaround. Another drawback of that arrangement was that the work was in another city, which meant we were constantly on the road and not as visible locally. Lately, much of that contract work has tapered off, and we find our calendar is still full.

Financially conservative: We know the old adage that "you have to spend money to make money" but have essentially disregarded it. Both of us are fiscally conservative, especially Pat. We discovered that fact early on in our business ventures and are satisfied that we followed the best path for our psychological well-being! While we might have been wealthier, we determined that peace of mind was more important. After reviewing our successes and shortfalls, we're still very comfortable with the process we follow and the outcomes we receive.

How to capitalize on your success factors and minimize your shortfalls

- Evaluate your location in terms of meeting your personal and professional goals. Pay special attention to the size of the community, the amenities for you and your family, and the ease of becoming involved and visible.
- Get involved in the community. Share your special expertise and talents on a volunteer basis. That can lead to a promotion and a more satisfying job offer and even provide contacts if you decide to start a business.
- Be adaptable as the community changes. Watch for trends. Ask your banker, accountant, attorney to let you know when they see changes occurring that might affect your employment or your business.
- If you're starting or sustaining a business, look for niche markets that are not being addressed by others. Sometimes you can piece together several small specialty areas rather than deal with large competitors in a major market arena.
- Seek input from others. You don't have to agree with their approach or act on their advice, but discussions can bring valuable new perspectives.
- Stay flexible to take advantage of new opportunities.
- Tailor your specialty areas to leverage your own style and strengths.
- Focus on your customer.
- Life is short. Make sure you enjoy what you're doing.

CHAPTER 9

Reinventing Ourselves

Celebrating successes with our client companies has always been one of our key motivators. When reviewing stories to include in this book, we realized that many of our most memorable and positive experiences occurred several years ago. It's not that current programs don't have successful outcomes, but we have noticed that participants tend to be more distracted, less engaged in the process, and generally don't appear to enjoy group activities or introspection as much as they once did.

Wondering if our content, delivery, or perspective had become less relevant, we discussed some of our observations with other facilitators and recent program participants. Their experiences echo our own. In reviewing the details of programs that were especially memorable, we noted the majority of those outstanding experiences took place *before* September 11, 2001. While aware of the profound effect that event had on people's attitudes and expectations, we assumed that life was gradually returning to the way it used to be. Now we understand that, in some ways, we Americans are still feeling the effects of that disaster.

Our musings led us to reflect on a brief survey that we conducted a couple of months after 9/11. We had been scheduled months earlier as presenters for the December 2001 session of the chamber of commerce's monthly breakfast briefing. In the aftermath of 9/11, we pondered how we could design and carry off that presentation since we are best known for our ability to accomplish important goals by using nonthreatening and lighthearted processes. This was certainly not the time for a lighthearted presentation.

We decided to conduct a quick, and admittedly unscientific, survey of our client companies to see what had changed in the two months since 9/11 and to use those findings as the basis for our presentation. We sent out e-mails to approximately seventy-five of our client companies asking each organization to answer a few focused questions. Since most companies were scrambling to deal with the aftermath of the event, we weren't optimistic about the number of responses we might receive and were surprised and gratified to receive a 73 percent response rate from our questionnaire. Here are a few of the things our clients had to say.

- 54 percent of the respondents had significantly changed their company policies in the areas of safety, security, and human resources
- 41 percent were experiencing significant slowdowns in their business
- 36 percent reported high levels of tension in the workplace
- Only 17 percent of our respondents thought that things would *ever* be the same as they were before the attacks.

One local CEO of a multinational organization commented that he thought America had "grown up" due to the events of 9/11 and people now realized that our country is a member of the global community—no longer immune to the terrorism that is regularly experienced in other parts of the world. In general, he expected an elevated feeling of suspicion and fear to permeate our work and personal lives for the foreseeable future.

As the effects of 9/11 played out in our country, vast changes were taking place throughout the world. A book published in July 2006 entitled *The New American Workplace* by James O'Toole and Edward Lawler III discusses current business trends and realities in the United States. The authors' conclusions echo many of our own observations. Our country faces ever-increasing worldwide competition, which now requires rapid and continuous change in products and strategies, more global operations, improved employee performance, and constant updating of skills.

Driven by the increase of global competition and fear of additional acts of terror, U.S. companies have rallied their employees to work harder and longer in order to remain competitive. Jobs have become more demanding with fewer employees handling the same, or increased, workloads. Add to that the movement of many manufacturing and customer service jobs to overseas locations, and the result is a very different workplace reality from that of five years ago. Personally, we see little loyalty on either side of the employee/ employer equation—a phenomenon which began with the huge downsizings of the last two decades and was exacerbated by the events of 9/11. Due to costs, time constraints, and frequent job hopping by employees, few companies offer much in the way of employee development except at the highest levels. We also see a workforce less inclined to value career advancement as much as personal freedom and flexibility.

Craig: Obviously, many of these changes have had an affect on our business. Like most organizations immediately after 9/11, we were concerned and uncertain about our future. We soon discovered that corporate training budgets had been redirected to security and disaster instruction. Fortunately, our history of working with upper level managers through outplacement and professional development processes was well known, and we began receiving calls to work with select individuals. Almost overnight, the focus of most of our consulting requests shifted from working with entire teams to helping individual executives and managers cope with the many complex issues they were now facing. In a way, our business had come full circle.

In addition to 9/11 events, the focus on electronics and technology has also changed the world of work. People are accessible electronically twenty-four hours a day and have come to expect work-related interruptions at almost any time. The dramatic impact of technology on interpersonal communication is all around us. People wander through grocery stores carrying on lengthy phone conversations. Students walk together in groups while talking on cell phones rather than to each other. And it's almost impossible to conduct any kind of meeting or one-on-one interaction without someone being interrupted by phone calls or text messages regardless of multiple requests to turn off or mute cell phones, PDAs, and beepers. People are more connected to information and less connected to personal interaction and relationships.

A popular newspaper columnist addressed this phenomenon as he recounted a recent travel experience. He was met at the airport by a limousine service. The driver held a card with the columnist's name on it. As the columnist approached his greeter, he realized the man was talking on his cell phone. Still engrossed in his conversation, the driver led the columnist to the limo, stowed his luggage, and settled into the driver's seat. The columnist checked his own phone messages and then listened to his iPod for the remainder of the trip. He paid the driver and, as he walked away, reflected on the sad fact that two people had spent over an hour in very close proximity without exchanging more than three or four words.

Pat: Changes in communication and interaction, the way businesses operate and view their employees, and our own assessment of the current corporate culture prompted us to ponder our own next steps. Over the past three to five years, our business has been primarily focused on coaching individuals and executive teams plus leadership development programming. Training provided for nonmanagement level employees is now mainly limited to technical subject matter rather than team and individual development, and we truly miss working with these groups and individuals.

Since most organizations now handle much of their training internally, we see a new niche for our skills and experience, enhancing the facilitation skills of group leaders and corporate trainers. To address that market, we have developed the process and materials to offer train-the-trainer seminars that target both corporate and freelance training professionals. A companion piece for trainers is our TAS, which is accessible for facilitators—both independent and corporate—to utilize with their own team processes.

We developed the survey about ten years ago when our specialty market was team building. Despite in-depth conversations with the executives, managers, or team leaders prior to our projects, we often uncovered issues during the program that would have been valuable to know about ahead of time. In many cases, the managers were either unaware of the issue or preferred to ignore it. Understandably, individual participants are often reluctant to publicly voice a concern about a sensitive topic. By using a confidential survey up front and combining all the data so statements are not attributable to any individual, a facilitator has all the information necessary to develop and deliver a meaningful program. The TAS results clearly identify the team's key issues, the extent to which the participants agree on the issues, and the amount of accord between management and the rest of the team. When assured of their anonymity and the confidentiality of their information, we find that team members readily share their opinions—both negative and positive.

After several years of experiencing the informational value the TAS lends to our program planning and delivery, we decided to investigate its scientific value. A local university analyzed our survey data for validity. That analysis revealed that the questions we had instinctively developed readily fell into six scientifically valid categories. We were somewhat surprised and extremely delighted to learn that our questionnaire provides more than just intuitive data. Using those six categories, we now provide our clients with data and bar graphs that compare their scores with those of the teams in the TAS database.

Additionally, teams can track their progress by comparing their scores at the beginning of the team building process with their scores when the process is completed. We are currently in the process of developing an Internet version of the survey for use by both corporate and external trainers.

Craig: We're excited about our next steps—training others to do the things we love to do, sharing our experiences, and drawing on the knowledge of program participants in return. Both of us enjoy telling stories and spreading the knowledge we've gained during more than twenty-eight years in the human resource business. In recounting our history for this book, we realized how many things have come full circle since our journey began.

- *We started out working with individuals, expanded our focus to work with large groups, and now find we're back to working with individuals and small executive teams.*
- *The business began with two people, we added numerous employees during the '80s and early '90s, and now it's just the two of us again.*
- *When we began our work, we used a handful of assessment instruments and gradually added more and more activities and props as the experiential business thrived. Now we're back to utilizing a few activities and assessments that have proven their value over the long term.*
- *We worked out of a home office the first year, ran three offices at the height of the outplacement boom, and now work from a home office once again.*

While our focus, our audience, our mode of delivery, and our work space have changed over the years, our beliefs, motives, philosophy, messages, and many of the tools we use have stood the test of time.

We are proof positive that you don't need lots of money, equipment, elaborate plans, or numerous employees to start and sustain a successful business. And today—with access to the Internet—starting an enterprise is easier than ever. If you have a burning desire and a good sense of the gifts and talents you have to share, you're well on your way. Whether running your own business or working for an organization, here's our advice:

- Do what energizes you.
- Offer something of value and be open to what others have to offer.

- Be flexible by adapting to time, place, needs, and situations.
- *Never* stop learning.
- Let others know what you stand for.
- Give back to your community and to the individuals who help you along the way.

A dream *can* become a reality—with or without three hundred bucks!

GLOSSARY

Terms

Team building—Programs and activities that demonstrate the premise that more can be accomplished by a group of people working together than by an individual.

Experiential Programming—Programs that encourage problem solving and generate insights and discussions through mental and/or physical challenges.

Executive Coaching—Working (usually one on one) with an individual to enhance skills required for success in executive level positions.

Facilitator Training—Training individuals or groups how to design and lead a variety of group programs.

Career Development Programming—Working with individuals or groups to enhance their self-knowledge and natural abilities enabling them to recognize and attain an ideal work situation.

High Ropes—Experiential activities that are performed on equipment (usually ropes or wires) elevated 6 or more feet off the ground. These are usually geared to individual performance although they may be part of a group program.

Low Ropes—Experiential activities for individuals or groups that take place on ropes or equipment that is slightly elevated. Successful completion of such an activity usually requires group input and cooperation.

Dutch Auction—An activity that involves groups in trying to win points by answering questions, finding resources, and/or performing certain activities. In the minds of the groups, it starts out as a competition (us against them), but they find out through trial and error that they can win more points if they find ways to collaborate or share with other groups.

Islands—A group outdoor activity that requires participants to work together to get the entire team from one platform to another without touching the ground.

Site Central—An activity that gets work teams to switch roles (executive and management, or groups from different divisions or different locations) and attempt to successfully complete a challenge. The premise is to actively demonstrate "walking in someone else's shoes."

Mute Lineup—A group of individuals must arrange themselves in correct order (i.e. by date of birth, name, etc.) without speaking.

Blind Square—A team is required to form a square with a large length of rope while blindfolded.

Nominal Group Technique—A group creates a list of options on cards or sticky notes and agrees upon the importance of each option through voting.

Nail Balance—Small groups of individuals are asked to balance ten penny nails on the head of one nail that is upright in a block of wood or Styrofoam.

Instruments

Myers-Briggs Type Indicator—Published by Consulting Psychologists Press. The MBTI instrument identifies an individual's degree of preference for four dichotomous dynamics. It is a trusted and widely used assessment for understanding individual differences and uncovering new ways to work and interact with others.

Leadership Practices Inventory—Published by Jossey-Bass. The LPI Observer is a thirty-item questionnaire used to rate leaders on The Five Practices® behaviors. The completed forms provide feedback from a variety of people—managers, direct reports, coworkers, and other colleagues who have had the opportunity to view the participant in leadership situations.

Team Assessment Survey—A validated questionnaire developed by The Rider Group to help teams identify their strengths and areas that need improvement. It consists of thirty-four forced choice and ten narrative questions. Teams use this data to target areas they wish to address. A key feature is that it can assess and compare the effectiveness of the team both before and after a teambuilding process. This data gives the team indicators of where they have improved and where they still need to focus.

Kuder Preference Test—Published by Science Research Associates Inc. Since 1939, the Kuder inventories have directed individuals toward making satisfying career choices.

Personal Strength Inventory—An in-depth, interview-based assessment developed by the Rider Group to help individuals find patterns that recur within accomplishments throughout their lifetime and in all areas of life. Knowing these gives individuals a clear way to describe the types of career situations that will engage their strengths and fit well with their unique pattern.

BIBLIOGRAPHY

Richard Nelson Bolles, **What Color Is Your Parachute?**, Ten Speed Press, published annually)

Steven Covey, **The Seven Habits of Highly Effective People,** (Simon & Schuster Inc., 1989)

James O'Toole and Edward Lawler III, **The New American Workplace,** Palgrave MacMillan, 2006

Dr. Marsha Sinetar**, Do What You Love, The Money Will Follow,** Paulist Press, 1987

INDEX